Some Unpublished Letters of Lord Chesterfield

PHILIP DORMER STANHOPE
EARL OF CHESTERFIELD

From an engraving after a painting by Gainsborough

SOME UNPUBLISHED

Letters of Lord Chesterfield

WITH AN INTRODUCTION BY
SIDNEY L. GULICK, JR.
ASSISTANT PROFESSOR OF ENGLISH
IN MILLS COLLEGE

University of California Press

Berkeley : 1937

UNIVERSITY OF CALIFORNIA PRESS
BERKELEY, CALIFORNIA

CAMBRIDGE UNIVERSITY PRESS
LONDON, ENGLAND

COPYRIGHT, 1937, BY THE
REGENTS OF THE UNIVERSITY OF CALIFORNIA

TO MY WIFE
WHO SHARED WITH ME
THE DISCOVERY OF THESE LETTERS

CONTENTS

	PAGE
Portrait of Lord Chesterfield . . . . . . *Frontispiece*	
From an engraving after a painting by Gainsborough	
Introduction	1
The Letters	19

	PAGE		PAGE		PAGE
I	19	X	34	XIX . . .	49
II	20	XI . . .	36	XX . . .	52
III . . .	22	XII . . .	38	XXI . . .	54
IV . . .	24	XIII . . .	41	XXII . .	56
V	26	XIV . . .	42	XXIII . .	58
VI . . .	28	XV . . .	43	XXIV . .	59
VII . . .	29	XVI . . .	44	XXV . .	61
VIII . . .	30	XVII . .	46	XXVI . .	63
IX . . .	32	XVIII . .	48		

Translation of Letter XXVI from the French of the original 70

"Thoughts" [Plan II] for the Future Education of his Godson 76

Index 83

INTRODUCTION

For all the great reputation of the fourth Earl of Chesterfield, few today read the bulk of his letters. A proper selection from his complete writings, cutting down the constant repetition of ideas—a repetition altogether necessary when he wrote the letters—may now seem preferable to any addition to the unread pages. Thus the publication of new letters requires a defense. What is there in the twenty-six letters in the present volume—fewer than one per cent of those already known—which justifies their presentation to the world?

To some, they will be interesting because they are new, but their significance grows from four factors: many of them were written late in Chesterfield's life and, together with the postscripts by Walsh, the amanuensis, they give new knowledge of the last six months; they show his mind, vital to the end, still seeing through sham and facing realities—"ni charlatan, ni dupe de charlatan"; combined with other material now first published, they give the evolution in Chesterfield's plans for the education of his godson; and finally, they sparkle, as all but his most pedagogic letters do, with comments on men and events. Thus, besides having bibliographical interest, they are extremely characteristic, filling out rather than changing one's conception of the Earl.

Before drawing conclusions from the new letters, it will be well to establish their authenticity. The Earl of Carnarvon, apparently after publishing Chesterfield's *Letters to his Godson* in 1890, had the originals inlaid in two sumptuously bound quarto volumes; following these, in the second volume, were inlaid the letters now published, together with miscellaneous other letters and documents, including the contract between Mrs. Eugenia Stanhope and James Dodsley for the publication of the *Letters to his Son*.[1] These two volumes are now in the possession of Mr. Arthur Zinkin, of Indianapolis, who has kindly given me permission to use them.[2]

Ten of the new letters are in Chesterfield's handwriting; the rest are dictated, but all are signed or initialed by the Earl. The amanuensis was James Walsh, Chesterfield's *valet de chambre;* in six of the letters, on the second or third page, is a postscript signed by Walsh, in the same handwriting as the dictated letter. A seventh letter by Walsh is on a separate sheet of paper.

Three drafts of Chesterfield's plan for the education of the godson, of which one is given in full and the others in extracts, are in the two thin volumes of manuscripts formerly belonging to the antiquarian, Evelyn Philip Shirley, who lent them to Lord Mahon when the latter was preparing his edition of Chesterfield (1845). These manuscripts are now in the possession of Dr. A. S. W. Rosenbach, by whose kindness they are used to illustrate Chesterfield's long letter to Deyverdun.

However, these letters scarcely need external proofs of genuineness, for in them characteristic phrases and ideas crop up frequently; the style is unmistakable. This being so, one may pass on to a brief sketch of the central figures and themes.

Above them all looms the Earl of Chesterfield himself,

---

[1] See *Publ. Mod. Lang. Assoc.*, LI:165–177 (March, 1936).

[2] Mr. Temple Scott, of New York, the well-known bibliophile and editor, bought these letters about 1928 for Mr. Jerome Kern, the New York collector, with the verbal understanding that Mr. Kern was not to offer them for public sale. Soon afterward, Mr. Scott sold them to Mr. Zinkin. A long article by Mr. Scott, in the *International Studio* for December, 1928, concerning the Jerome Kern collection, includes a description of the two volumes.

who is too well known to need here an extended account of his life and works.* Born in 1694 and coming into the earldom in 1726, through his many activities Chesterfield became acquainted with most of the well-known men of nearly a century: when a boy, he saw Richard Cromwell, the son of the Protector; he lived thirteen years into the reign of George III. All the political figures for half a century were his friends or opponents. Among the literati he knew Addison, Pope, and Swift; he disappointed Johnson. He was at home in the salons of Paris and was the acknowledged master of English society.

Although never of the importance or power of Sir Robert Walpole, the Duke of Newcastle, or William Pitt,—successively the leaders of Parliament during his career,—Chesterfield played an honorable part in the political life of his time. Twice Ambassador to Holland (1728–1732 and 1745), he was each time conspicuously successful. In the interim, as one of the leaders of the Opposition, he was noted for the wit and satire of his orations in Parliament and of his political essays in *Fog's Journal, Common Sense,* and *Old England.* His Lord-Lieutenancy of Ireland, although of only a few months' duration, came at the tense moment of the rebellion of '45, which was not far from succeeding in England. A Roman Catholic country, oppressed, misgoverned, harshly taxed, Ireland had every reason to support the Young Pretender. Yet Chesterfield ruled with such wise restraint and firmness that he could even spare troops for

---

* The best full-length life is by Bonamy Dobrée, appearing as the introduction to his edition of Chesterfield's *Letters* (1932); lives by William Ernst (1893), W. H. Craig (1907), and Samuel Shellabarger (1935) are respectively dull, inaccurate, and written to support a thesis. Excellent sketches are by Charles Strachey, in the *Letters to his Son* (1901), and by Lord Carnarvon, in the *Letters to his Godson* (1890).

service in England. His apparent promotion to be co-Secretary of State with the Duke of Newcastle, in 1746, proved a delusion. The Duke kept all the important business in his own hands, merely making capital out of Chesterfield's well-known probity, for in a notoriously venal age he took no bribes, sold no offices, and kept his word. For a time Chesterfield believed that he could outlast the blundering, indefatigable Newcastle. In February, 1748, worn out by vain opposition to policies he knew were wrong, Chesterfield resigned his office, and virtually retired from politics. His last great speech came three years later, when he carried through the House of Lords the bill for the reform of the calendar. Soon after, the deafness which had already been troubling him increased, and cut him off from the pleasures of society and conversation, as well as from politics.

Chesterfield's interests were by no means confined to the affairs of government. Among his wide acquaintanceship he took pride in knowing men of letters. A liberal patron of many a hack writer aspiring for fame, he received numerous dedications and much fulsome praise, tokening benefits in hand or hoped for. His known generosity led Samuel Johnson, then celebrated chiefly as the author of *London*,—for which he had received ten guineas from the publisher,—to make use of his name as an excuse for delay in presenting Robert Dodsley with the Plan for his dictionary.[4] Chesterfield rewarded him with a gift of ten pounds.[5] Johnson's disappointment at receiving no further attention until the *Dictionary* was ready for publication precipitated the famous letter which has unjustly done much to smirch Chesterfield's name.

---

[4] Boswell's *Life of Johnson* (ed. G. B. Hill; Oxford, 1887), I, 183.
[5] *Ibid.*, 261 n. 3.

INTRODUCTION 5

But if pilloried in Boswell's *Life of Johnson,* Chesterfield is remembered for his *Letters to his Son.* Written in confidence to his only son, obviously in a father's urgency that his son attain distinction, upon the death of both son and father they were exhibited to the public with the most casual of editing. The acclaim with which they were first received soon gave way to adverse criticism. The *Letters* were advertised as a complete system of education, whereas in reality they were counsel to a studious and retiring boy to learn the ways of society, to shine by good manners; and in the course of a few months certain passages urging, as a desperate measure to teach these manners, the forming of a *liaison* with a married Frenchwoman raised a storm of abuse the echoes of which still reverberate. Much has been written on this subject; perhaps the best defense of the Earl is that the publication of these letters violated a confidence and that he was only expressing frankly what in his time was common practice. Aside from these few regrettable passages, the *Letters* contain chiefly the advice of a worldly wise man of affairs, written in a style that has made them a classic.

These letters were addressed to Philip Stanhope, the Earl's illegitimate son. Before the son's death in 1768, the Earl had already begun the education of another Philip Stanhope, who was to succeed him as the fifth Earl of Chesterfield. A long series of letters to this youth was published in 1890 by the Earl of Carnarvon; the present collection adds to that series. The earliest of the new letters, written in 1761, came after Chesterfield had retired from politics and from society; his deafness had long troubled him acutely. The first seven letters may quickly be dispersed among the many in Lord Carnarvon's edition and then dismissed. The remainder of the letters, particularly the sixteen dictated ones dating from August, 1772, to March 7, 1773 (seventeen days before the Earl's death), give the ebb and flow of his last days: in his seventy-ninth year, he knew the end was close.

When he could no longer hold a pen himself, his *valet de chambre,* James Walsh, wrote from his dictation. To Walsh, besides all his clothes and wearing apparel, Chesterfield by his will left an annuity for life of eighty pounds, accompanying it with one of twenty pounds to Walsh's son Jemmy. The postscripts from Walsh to the godson show on what familiar terms they were; the matter indited shows what trust Chesterfield put in Walsh.

As to the godson,—one more of many bearing the name Philip Stanhope,—it is superfluous to add to Lord Carnarvon's account. Born in 1755, he lived undistinguished until 1815. Lord Carnarvon (p. lxxi) remarked on the contrast between the boy's accomplishment and the old Earl's hopes for him that he would shine in courts and make a figure in Parliament. Had the Earl a premonition that his godson would not distinguish himself? In one letter printed by Carnarvon,[6] referring to the extravagance of the young Earl of Carlisle, there was a hint that Chesterfield feared the boy's giddiness; there was more than a hint in his will: to prevent his successor from squandering the wealth which he felt necessary to support an earldom, Chesterfield entailed the estate, even to the "household goods, plate, statues, bustoes, vases, books, pictures, and furniture"—a pretty complete catalogue. Furthermore, as is well known, he provided for a forfeit of £5000 should the godson ever keep a pack of hounds, take part in horse racing, go during the races to Newmarket, "that infamous seminary of iniquity and ill man-

---

[6] The next to the last.—Dobrée, VI, 2919.

ners," or lose as much as £500 in any one day through gaming or betting. Whatever love Chesterfield had for his godson, he did not trust his frugality or his judgment.

More fully than these, however, the last letters show Chesterfield to have had few illusions left concerning the boy. He was on friendly terms with his seventeen-year-old ward, praising, exhorting, counseling; but here and there in the last six months, as the reader may find without searching, he writes with a trenchancy which shows that his mind did not fail with his health. In the very last letter of all, written only seventeen days before his death, there is no scolding or recrimination, but resignation. Chesterfield had frequently expressed a willingness for negative health; now he seems ready to accept a negatively decent successor.

To this end had years of effort come. Ill-chosen tutors and governors were in part to blame; the general poor quality of education, much; the subject, perhaps more. Of the earlier schoolmasters there is no reason to speak; mediocre they certainly were, although it might have been hard to know that at the time. But when the boy was sent to the care of Dr. William Dodd, that man had an irreproachable reputation. Chesterfield was expressing the general opinion when in 1765 he wrote that Dodd was "the best and most eloquent preacher in England, and perhaps the most learned clergyman."[7] In October, 1770, as these new letters indicate, Chesterfield still held Dr. Dodd in high regard; a break of twenty-two months in the correspondence unfortunately obscures events which one is curious to know. Whatever happened, by August, 1772, Chesterfield had changed his mind about Dr. Dodd, and the subsequent letters show that rather be-

---
[7] June 5, 1765.

fore the general opinion of the eloquent clergyman fell, the Earl had smoked him out. Unfortunately, this occurred after the boy had "lost entirely, with regard to learning, the two best years" of his life. The letters of October to December, 1772, glitter with gossip about the Dodds. In spite of this, when he came into his estate, the young Earl gave Dodd the living of Wing in Buckinghamshire.[8] The subsequent events are familiar history: when Dodd forged his name to a bond for £4200,[9] the boy testified that the signature was not his. Notwithstanding appeals and petitions, in which Dr. Johnson took an active part, Dodd was hanged.[10]

The other tutor mentioned in these letters was of a different stamp: Georges Deyverdun, a Swiss man of letters who was Edward Gibbon's lifelong friend. When in 1753, at the age of sixteen, Gibbon was sent to Lausanne, he soon met Deyverdun, some two years his elder, "a young man of an amiable temper and excellent understanding." In England, years afterward, the two collaborated in producing *Mémoires Littéraires de la Grande Bretagne*, for 1767 and 1768; the second of these was dedicated to Chesterfield (April 12, 1769). Twenty months later, when he came to the problem of who should be the godson's governor, Chesterfield wrote, "I know one M. Deyverdun of Lausanne ... who I think would answer this purpose; he has a great deal of useful polite learning, with almost the manners of a gentleman."[11]

---

[8] *Gentleman's Magazine*, XLVII (1777), 340.

[9] The godson, by an interesting coincidence, had drawn on Chesterfield for exactly this sum during the first nine months of his trip abroad; for Chesterfield's comment, see Letter XXV.

[10] *Papers Written by Dr. Johnson and Dr. Dodd*, by R. W. Chapman (Oxford, 1926); also Boswell's account, under date of September, 1777.

[11] See below, p. 80, for this passage in its context.

INTRODUCTION

Thus Deyverdun became the governor of the boy, although, as Gibbon remarked in his memoirs, "In a residence of several years, he never acquired the just pronunciation and familiar use of the English tongue." This lack was of small consequence, for he had not been engaged to teach English to his pupil. On July 26, 1771, Chesterfield completed his long letter of instructions to Deyverdun, first published in the present collection; the envelope was inscribed: "This to be given to Monsieur D'ayverdun. In case I should dye before he returns, and before he goes abroad with my Godson." But the Earl lived, and the letter was kept among his papers. In June, 1772, the two set out for Leipzig, where they remained, apparently, until the next summer (Chesterfield died in March), returning to Leipzig again in the autumn. In September, Gibbon declined to edit Chesterfield's letters to his illegitimate son, since "the family were strongly bent against it; and especially on Deyverdun's account, I deemed it more prudent to avoid making them my personal enemies." According to the *Gentleman's Magazine*,[12] Dr. Dodd saw the godson in Geneva in the summer of 1774; presumably Deyverdun was no longer with him, for on April 21, 1774, Gibbon mentioned that he was shortly to set out with Lord Middleton.

Subsequently, one may note that when in 1783 Gibbon retired to Lausanne, the two old friends lived together until Deyverdun's death on July 4, 1789.[13]

Lord Chesterfield's plan for the education of his godson was not greatly unlike that for his son: study under

---
[12] XLVII (1777), 340.
[13] Quérard, *La France Littéraire*, is useful chiefly in giving Deyverdun's dates and referring one to Gibbon, from whose *Memoirs of My Life and Writings* and *Letters*—here quoted from the *Miscellaneous Works* (London, 1837)—most of the foregoing is taken: pages 36, 86, 257, 258, 259, 263.

competent teachers in England until the age of fifteen or so, to be followed by further study in various places on the Continent. But although the son spent some time in Italy, even the earliest record of Chesterfield's plan for his godson—published with the letters to the boy's father, A. C. Stanhope[14]—absolutely bans that country, as do the three Plans mentioned below, the letter to Deyverdun, and, latest of them all, Chesterfield's will. The terms vary but little from one to another. Bad morals made the country abhorrent to the Earl. What! in his old age did the Earl reform? That is what Lord Carnarvon believed, for he felt that in the letters to the godson "a somewhat higher moral tone may be distinguished" than in the letters to the son. He added, "It is generous as well as fair to take note that the twenty years which had elapsed since the passages that were so worthy of blame were written, had produced certain changes" (pp. lv, lvi). Mr. Bonamy Dobrée, in his recent edition of Chesterfield's letters, doubted the change (I, 208–210), remarking that Chesterfield's suggestions were probably governed by the specific situation rather than by any change of heart; Mr. Dobrée was right. The letter to Deyverdun authorized him to interfere only if an affair became shameful and dishonorable, or affected the boy's health. It was unnatural attachments, and music, of which Chesterfield was afraid in Italy.

Although the various plans are in general much the same, one can trace gradual changes in Chesterfield's ideas, and, furthermore, through the changes one can fix the order of the undated plans. The dated plans mark the limits in time: the earliest is that in the letter to A. C. Stanhope, dated October 1, 1762; the latest is the letter

---

[14] Letter of October 1, 1762.

in French to Deyverdun, first printed in this volume, dated July 26, 1771.[15]

Not to pause over the order of the earlier Plans, a comparison of them with the letter to Deyverdun shows surprising similarities, so much so that in the translation the best idiom is frequently to be found in Chesterfield's own words, written some years earlier. In my translation, accordingly, where these phrases can be used, they appear enclosed in angles, thus: < >. Much more frequently there is a rough parallelism which does not permit Chesterfield's exact English phraseology. A comparison of the letter to Deyverdun with Plan II, which is printed in full, and with the illustrative passages from Plans I and III, will show how strongly, over a period of years, Chesterfield's mind ran in the same channel and very nearly in the same words. In these parallels there is no indication that he had in mind one particular earlier draft, for in writing to Deyverdun he repeated phrases unique to each

[15] Of the three in Dr. Rosenbach's collection (which I label Plan I, Plan II, and Plan III, but which are inserted among the MSS in the order II, I, III), Plan III, written by an amanuensis and signed by Chesterfield, is dated December 25, 1770. The other two are undated. The clearest index to the order of these plans is the age at which the godson was to be sent on his travels. In the letter to A. C. Stanhope, the boy was to be 14 or 15; in Plan I, he was to be sent at 15; in Plan II, he was to stay at Dr. Dodd's until near 16; in Plan III, he was to go in April, 1772, when he would be 16½: actually, he left in June, 1772. Thus the boy's travels were little by little postponed as the time drew near. The development of Chesterfield's ideas concerning a governor for the boy is another key to the order of the Plans: Plans I and II can hardly be reversed. The brief French sketch of a course of study, accompanying the letter to A. C. Stanhope and said to be "drawn up by the Earl for the direction of the studies of this youth, when he went abroad some years afterwards," certainly preceded Plan III, for it mentions Geneva as the boy's destination, whereas in Plan III and the letter to Deyverdun the destination is Leipzig, where the boy actually went. Plan II must have been written after February 8, 1766, when Philip Stanhope went to Dr. Dodd's; how much after, the internal evidence does not show. Plan I may have come either before or after this date, but in any case preceded Plan II.

of them. Moreover, the frequent difference in phrasing, as for example in his opinions regarding Italy, would indicate that he did not have the former drafts before him when he wrote the later ones and the letter to Deyverdun.

The significant changes from 1762 to 1771 are three: first, in respect to when the boy should begin his travels, second, where he should go, and third, how he should be governed. In the earliest plan, that enclosed in the letter to A. C. Stanhope, he was to leave in 1769 or 1770—that is, at the age of fourteen or fifteen—and spend three years in Geneva, after which a stay of one year in Paris was to be followed by a trip home through Flanders and Holland. In this he was to have no governor, but be under the strict authority of a professor of belles-lettres in Geneva. In Plan I, he was to leave England at the age of fifteen, spend three years in Geneva, two in Paris, five months at The Hague, and travel through Germany, perhaps rapidly passing through Petersburg, Copenhagen, and Stockholm after he became of age. In all these countries he was to see the courts, not the countrysides. A proper Genevan governor, Chesterfield thought, might be found for the boy—certainly not an Englishman. His travels through Germany, Holland, and the north remained approximately the same in the later plans. In Plan II, he was to start a year later, and thus be limited to one year in Paris. Here Chesterfield's ideas of a governor were somewhat expanded: a tolerably well-bred Swiss or Genevan, and by no means "an English parson or Scotch doctor of physic." In Plan III, the boy was to start still later (in April, 1772, at sixteen and a half), and go first to Leipzig for six or seven months, after which might follow six months in Geneva. After this one year of preliminary study (in place of the three of the previous plans), the boy would go to

Paris for two years. In this plan Deyverdun is first named. The letter to Deyverdun, written six months later,—and incidentally as long as any two of the other plans,—finally omitted Geneva altogether. One year in Leipzig was to be followed by six months in some provincial town of France—substituted for Geneva because less infested with the boy's compatriots—before, at the age of eighteen, he was to be exposed to the dangers of Paris. There he should stay a full year, after which travels in Germany, Holland, and the north would occupy two years more. Deyverdun, in the humorous reference to *Candide,* was delicately instructed, as Chesterfield expressed it in Plan III, not to be "inseparably joined to him like an unnatural birth."

But good wine needs no bush, and neither do Chesterfield's felicities and pungencies of expression. It remains, then, only necessary to explain the principles upon which the texts have been edited. Where large quantities of manuscript are concerned, orthographical peculiarities should not be preserved, since they retard the ordinary reader, and tend to discourage him. But with a figure so important in the literary history of a period as Lord Chesterfield, it is proper that a small portion of his writings should appear with literal accuracy. The photographic reproduction of one letter is scarcely adequate, even though as perfect as in Lord Carnarvon's edition. Therefore, the number of holograph letters in this collection being few, I have striven for literal accuracy, although in some respects with doubtful success. For example, particularly in the letter to Deyverdun, it is at times impossible to determine whether Chesterfield wrote L or l, S or s, J or j, for there are all gradations between the capital and the small letter. Further, in his frequent use of I where now one writes J, there is also an intermediate letter. Cancellations are indicated thus [*canc.:* the word or words cancelled] and interlineations thus [*interl.:* the word or words interlineated].

With respect to the dictated letters, I have felt impelled to normalize; two short samples will justify my action:

"I imagine You, at this moment, starring in the town of Liepzig, taking a liker of the Professors, and They of You, but You, will I hope, See Them, with more attention, then They will bestow upon You, for You must be conscious, that between Dr. Dodd's great negligence, and your own Idleness, you have lost, intirely, with regard to learning, the two best Years of your life."

"The Musick you sent for, will get to You as soon as possible, but It is. Because you say It is for a Lady, for you know, that when we parted, you promised me, never to turn, piper or Fidler."

This much will also serve to indicate the habits of the amanuensis, and under what difficulty Lord Chesterfield indited his letters. One can imagine the old Earl, from his bed watching the intent Walsh slowly form his neat letters; at each pause in the dictation the pen would scratch in a comma: "... the Professors, and They of You, but You, will I hope, See Them, with more attention, then They will bestow upon you...." Walsh's own postscripts to the godson, although also requiring to be normalized, have less excess punctuation; the phrasing is then that of dictation, and where the phrases are excessively short, as in part of the two examples given above, Chesterfield was possibly speaking under some difficulty. However that may be, not only did Walsh punctuate without consistency and always overpunctuate; he capitalized at every whim. In spelling, he was perversely consistent: *then* for

INTRODUCTION

than, loose for *lose, gaurd* for *guard,* and once *laying* for *lying.* On this account I have corrected his misspellings, with the exception of proper names only when they are unidentified or are at once given correctly in a footnote. His paragraphing, which is not always logical, is nevertheless unaltered; but not to normalize the rest would be to make the letters needlessly difficult to read.

As separate envelopes were not then generally used for letters, the fourth page, left blank for the purpose, took the address; this is given wherever it is found, with, however, normalized spelling in the dictated letters. The recipient frequently broke the seal carelessly, tearing out a word or more from page three—repeatedly the cause for lacunae to be supplied from the context. These are invariably indicated by square brackets and a footnote; words omitted in the writing but necessary for the sense are supplied in square brackets without a footnote.

S. L. G.

THE LETTERS

[I]

[Before July 28, 1761][16]*

My Dear Godson.

I am told that you are the best boy in the world, and that you love learning, and Know more than any boy in England of your age. This makes me love you, and will make every body else love, and admire you.

If we were together we would play mightily; sometimes at Shuttlecock, sometimes at books, sometimes at Ball, and sometimes at Globes. I am told too that you are [*interl.:* a] boy of honour, and never tell a lye upon any account whatsoever. I will therefore every now and then send you some pretty things to play with; and particularly I will send you a watch, as soon as ever you write to me your self for one. Good night My Dear.

Chesterfield

To Master Philip Stanhope.[17]

---

* Notes to the letters will be found following the particular letters to which they refer.

[16] This letter precedes the earliest printed by Lord Carnarvon (in the *Letters to his Godson*), which is dated July 28.

[17] The outside address; see Introduction, p. 15.

[II]

Black-heath. Augst 20 1761

Mon chér Filleul.

I am very glad that you are so well pleased with your watch, I assure you I am extremely pleased with your letter, which is still better wrote than your former, and [*interl.:* I] read it at sight, which, I will lay you a wager is more than you can do your watch. Do you know the progress of the minute hand, and can you tell when it is at so many minutes after any hour? I believe you know that there [*interl.:* are] sixty minutes in an hour, and sixty seconds in a minute, but I do not believe that you [*interl.:* know] the figures of the inmost circle which are called Roman figures, nor the figures of the outermost circle, which are called Arabick figures; as for instance, nine in Roman figures is marked thus IX, but in the Arabick figures thus 9. I believe you will think writing to me once a month very troublesome, but do not hate me for it, because I require it only for your good, for I am sure you will do your best when you write to me, and the pleasure of doing well, is worth any trouble it may cost. Would you grudge any trouble to excell all other boys of your age? I dare say you would not. I am told that you read extremely well, which I can tell you is more difficult than writing well. But what do you read? I fancy you read the little History of England which I sent you some time ago, and that you are perfectly well acquainted with William the Conqueror, who conquered England about seven hundred years ago, and also with Edward the third and his son, the black Prince who together almost conquered France, as likewise with Henry the fifth who quite conquered it, and was crowned King of France at Paris, which you know is the capital Town of France. I am glad that you like reading, it is a very good amusement, but you must give yourself time to play, and at games of much exercise, which will make you strong and healthy. When you play, play with all your heart, and think of nothing else, and when you read, do the same, and think of nothing but what you read. Il ne faut Jamais étre paresseux ni oisif, il faut toujours faire quelque chose, car L'oisiveté est la Mére de tous les vices. Adieu, vous étes un bon petit garçon.

[III]

London. Sept: y̆e 16th 1761

Petit Garçon.

You are a little boy, and why should not I call you so? You may if you please call me a little man in return; it is none of my fault, I have wished myself taller a thousand times, but to no purpose, for all the Stanhopes are but a size above dwarfs. But little as you may be as a Boy, I find that you are a very able Man in Politicks, for when a whole Kingdom is pulled to pieces and disjoynted, you can by your superior skill unite and set all right again. Who could have thought it? You see what attention and application will bring about. I see by your writing, that you do not want either, for you improve in it extremely. You seem to challenge me before it be long in the History of England, and therefore I am studying it very hard in order to be ready for you. I observe among the pictures of the Kings of England, Henry the VIII broad face to be very like yours. But I would not advise you to be like him in any other respect, for he was a Brutal Tyrant. He had six wives one after another, of whom he cut off the heads of two, and put away two others, only because he did not like them. It is true he was the cause of establishing the Protestant Religion in this Kingdom, but not from good motives. His daughter Queen Elizabeth, whose picture you have, to be sure seen with a great Ruff about her [*interl.:* neck], finished that good work. She was a great woman. But not content it seems with putting this whole Kingdom in good order, you have an eye to the affairs of the fabulous world contained in Ovid's Metamorphosis [*sic*]. Upon my word you have a great deal of business upon your hands; but so much the better, for nothing is so bad as Lazyness and Idleness. Besides that when you go to a great School, not only the Master, but the boys will admire you, for having so much knowledge. And what a pleasure must it be to you to be put over the heads of many boys older than yourself? I am glad that your Papa has found benefit by bathing at Buxton.[18] You seem to be very well with him, and I hope he is so with you. I hope I am so too, car vous êtes un tres bon garçon, ét c'est pourquoy Je vous aime beaucoup. Adieu.

To Philip Stanhope Esqre
  at Mansfield in
    Nottinghamshire
Free
Chesterfield

---

[18] Buxton, in Derbyshire, the highest town in England, a health resort with thermal and chalybeate baths.

[IV]

Bath. Decem: yͤ 2ᵈ 1761

You are positively the best boy in the world, and at this rate we shall grow proud of you, and you grow Justly proud of your self; for though none but fools are proud of birth or rank,[19] sensible people may and will be proud of superior merit, and knowledge. I see you have a good and quick memory, and as memory is acquired by attention, and [*interl.:* preserved and] improved by frequent exercise, I will find exercise enough for yours. I send you therefore a very pretty copy of verses of Mʳ Waller's,[20] which he sent with a Rose to a Lady. They are in a different measure from the last I sent you [*canc.:* but] which [*canc.:* are; *interl.:* were] what are called long verses, that is of ten Syllables each line.

> Go lovely Rose,
>   Tell her who wastes her time and me,
> That now she knows
>   When I ressemble her to thee,
> How sweet and fair, she seems to be.
>
> Tell her who's young,
>   And shuns to have her Graces spyed,
> That had'st thou sprung,
>   In deserts where no men abide,
> Thou must have uncommended dyed.
>
> Then dye, that she,
>   The common fate of all things rare
> May read in thee,
>   How small a part of time they share,
> That are so wond'rous sweet and fair.

In my next I will send you some more; but do not hurry your self to get these by heart, for I would have you do nothing that you do not do with pleasure and attention. And so good night to your honour, or in French, Je vous donne le bon soir Monsieur.

To Philip Stanhope Esqre.

---

[19] Compare Horace Walpole's letter to Sir Horace Mann, September 1, 1750 (*Letters*, edited by Mrs. Paget Toynbee, III, 11): "... but I am now grown to bear no descent but my Lord Chesterfield's, who has placed among the portraits of his ancestors two old heads, inscribed *Adam de Stanhope* and *Eve de Stanhope;* the ridicule is admirable."

[20] Chesterfield omitted the second stanza:

> Small is the worth
>   Of beauty from the light retired;
> Bid her come forth,
>   Suffer herself to be desired,
>   And not blush so to be admired.

He also substituted *who* for *that* in the second and sixth lines.

[V]

London Jan: ye 2^d 1762

Dear Godson.

I find it goes better and better every day; your last letter was better writt than your former, and at this rate when we meet, I believe I had best borrow your hand to write for me, as mine grows weaker, and yours grows stronger every day. You have I perceive, a ready memory to have got by heart all the verses I have sent you, and therefore to exercise it, I will here send you a few more, of the same Poet Mr Waller. Not that I suppose you can understand all the delicacy of them at present, but as by getting them by heart so young, you will always remember them, you will, in four or five years be able to taste all their beautys, and I will send you none but the best Authors.

Now I will tell you some good news concerning your self. Your Lottery Tickett is come up a prize. It is not indeed the 10000^L, nor the 5000^L, nor a 1000^L, nor yet 100^L, but it is a whole twenty pounds prize, which [*interl.:* is] an instance of your present, and an earnest of your future good fortune.[21]

Make my compliments to your Father, and tell him that I have been laid up this week with most exquisite pain, but whether from the Gout or a Rheumatism, the skillfull have not yet decided.[22]

I wish you all many happy new years, and as for your little self, if you turn out a learned and an honest Man, you can never be unhappy, let what will happen. A good conscience is the best security for happyness. And so, God bless you.

I had almost forgot to put you in mind to chuse King

and Queen on twelfth night, and likewise to eat a whole minced pye for your share.[23]

ON A LADY'S GIRDLE.

That which her slender waist confined,
Shall now my Joyfull temples bind.
No Monarch but would give his Crown,
His Arms might do what this has done.[24]

A Narrow compass; and yet there
Dwells all that's lovely, all that's fair.
Give me but what this ribband bound,
Take all the rest the Sun goes round.

Remember however that Mr Waller was a better Poet, than he was an Astronomer, for the Sun does not go round, it is fix'ed, and it is this globe the Earth, that goes round the sun.[25]

---

[21] According to the *Gentleman's Magazine* for December, 1761 (XXXI, 602), the first prize, of £10,000, "was the property of an industrious man, who had laboured hard for 40 years, and could but barely live by his business. He had been told that his ticket had been unfortunate, and was come to sell the blank, when he was agreeably surprized with the news of its being the £10,000 prize."

[22] This attack lasted some months; according to Maty (*Miscellaneous Works* of Lord Chesterfield [1779], I, 345 n.), the disease was rheumatism.

[23] Traditionally, the Christmas festivities ended on Twelfth Night, when—according to one custom—a cake with a bean or tiny doll in it was cut and the pieces distributed, to determine the monarch of the revels; the person getting the token would choose a partner, and the two would be King and Queen. Mince pie was also a traditional dish of the season. See Chambers' *Book of Days*, under January 6 and December 25.

[24] Chesterfield again omits a second stanza:

> It was my heaven's extremest sphere,
> The pale which held that lovely deer.
> My joy, my grief, my hope, my love,
> Did all within this circle move!

[25] Concerning his famous speech on reforming the calendar, Chesterfield wrote (February 28, 1751) to his son: "I was obliged to talk some astronomical jargon, of which I did not understand one word, but got it by heart, and spoke it by rote from a master."

[VI]

janȳ 17. 1763. Lundi Matin.

Je languis de te revoir Mon cher petit drôle, et peut être a tu envie de me revoir. Mais comment faire? Je ne puis sortir, et Je crains ta sortie dans le tems qu'il fait,[26] Mais si vous n'étes pas enrhumme, et que Monsieur Robert[27] croit que vous pouvis sortir impunément [*canc.:* sortir]. J'enverray mon Carosse demain a Midi vous chercher, et vous dinerez avec moy. Adieu.

To Master Philip
Stanhope.

---

[26] According to the *Annual Register* for 1762 (pp. 119–120) there was severely cold weather in England from December 25 to January 29, with ice on the Severn six feet thick in places.

[27] The editor of the *Letters to A. C. Stanhope* (1817; p. viii) styled Robert: "... a dissipated Frenchman, ... who kept an academy at Marybone, from whence he removed to a large house near Vauxhall, where he lived very extravagantly, and at last sunk into poverty." The godson went to him before the middle of July, 1762, and stayed until February, 1766.

[VII]

Au bout du compte il faut quelquefois se divertir, et pas toujours s'appliquér, c'est pourquoy Je vous envoye ce livre qui vous amusera beaucoup, sur tout comme vous aves du gout pour le dessein. Ce sont des tailles douces de toutte L'Histoire Sacrée et prophane.

Sachez que L'Histoire Sacrée veut dire L'Histoire de la Bible, et L'Histoire prophane veut dire, les contes a dormir debout des Payens, qu'on appelle La Fable. Ce sont des Jolis mensonges qui sont pour la pluspart contenus dans les Metamorphoses d'Ovide. Il n'est que Juste de commençér par la verité, qui est L'Histoire de L'escriture Sainte dont Je vous envoye ce premier Volume. Lisez les trois ou quatre lignes qui sont au bas de chaque Planche, et qui vous expliqueront de quoy il est question. Quand vous vous seréz assez diverti avec ce Volume, Je vous en enverray un autre. Adieu petit bout d'homme, Je t'embrasse.

Jeudi.[28]

To Master Stanhope.

---

[28] March 3, 1763 (?), the Thursday preceding March 8, 1763, when Chesterfield mentioned the illustrated history in a letter to A. C. Stanhope.

[VIII]

Bath Oct ye 6th 1770

My Dear Son.

Non semper arcum tendit Apollo;[29]
he has a great deal of different business to do, and cannot come at every call; The Muses too being ladys are consequently a little whimsical and capricious, and will not come like prostitutes [*canc.:* at every call] whenever called upon. There is in all things a favourable moment, the *Mollia tempora,*[30] which should be seized and enjoyed but can never be forced. I content my self with your letters in prose, till you are *aflatus Lumine*[.] The greatest Poets, Dryden, Addison, and Pope, have not been always equally inspired any more than you.

I am glad to hear of your restoration at Sr William Stanhope's's[31] because I know it depended upon Dr Dodd's testimony, who[32] is always a willing witness in your favour and without whose Character no body will take you. Be convinced once for all that the Doctor and I can have no interest but yours, in all our representations of what we would have you do, or not do, and I leave you to Judge who is the most capable of it, your inexperience at fifteen or my experience at seventy six.

Your notions of the crueltys and devastations of war are very Just though not fashionable, for on the contrary when two or three silly Kings quarrel from their respective Closets, it is both Just and glorious that myriads of their Subjects, better in some . . . . .[33] respects than themselves, should be the Victims of their differences; I still believe and hope that we shall have no war[.] France and

Spain are not yet ripe for one, and I hope our Ministers do not, for I am sure they have not abilitys to carry it on. You seem to wonder that the people desire one, but I will tell you that that is the Characteristick of the people every where, they always wish for what they have not, besides they love events to amuse or rouse their animal spirits, and war is more productive of events than peace.

There is very little, I may say, no good company yet. There are some Irish bloods, and some English Bucks of the adjacent Counties, the formidable looks of the former especially when their hats are on almost tempt me to swear the peace against them, and as for the Bumpkins, in their Deer skin Waistcoats, Postilions Caps, a pair of couples hanging at their belts, and a hunting whip about their shoulders, they are only formidable to the beasts they hunt, except by their Spurs to the petty coats in the publick rooms. Your friend Garrick is the only Man here whom I am, or desire to be acquainted with, he calls you his Champion, and always makes very honourable mention of you. I am very glad of it, for I think and I hope you do, that distinguished merit in any way, is better than rank without it. God bless you. Do all you can to be *Memmius*,[34] you may be it if you please.

---

[29] Neque semper arcum tendit Apollo.—Horace, *Odes*, II, x, 19-20.

[30] Perhaps Chesterfield's recollection of Virgil's
...mollissima fandi tempora.—*Aeneid*, IV, 293-4.

[31] At this time, Sir William Stanhope (1702-1772) was Chesterfield's only surviving brother.

[32] For Dr. William Dodd, see the Introduction, pp. 7-8.

[33] A cancelled word is here undecipherable.

[34] Gaius Memmius (died *ca.* 49 B.C.), the Roman orator and poet to whom Lucretius addressed the *De Rerum Natura*. See Chesterfield's reference to Memmius in the letter of November 5, 1766.

[IX]

Bath Oct: 16 1770

Dear Son.

Yesterday I received your letter, which savours too strongly of that Idle state of dissipation which you have of late been in, for your lines are neither paralel nor horizontal but Diagonal.[35] The Chinese write perpendicularly from the top to the bottom of the paper, some other Nations write from the right to the left, but I know no grown up people who write diagonally except your self, and perhaps the Duke of Cumberland.[36] This proceeds from your hurry, and your want to do some nothing or other, for whoever has eyes can write their lines straight if they please and it is very awkward not to do it. I do not like your frequent excursions which have lost you so many mornings, that is so many days, for serious solid Studys are only the business of the morning. Could Edwyn Stanhope's[37] parenthesis make you any Amends for what you lost of Horace, Cicero or Sophocles? For God's sake consider how precious your time ought to be to you now; I am sure I do not say too much when I tell you that one week's study now, is worth three months, three or four years hence to you. These migrations and excursions are now, thanks to the season, pretty well over, and my Brother with his horde now camps at Tilney hall,[38] and in a short time settles in Town. Next year these things must not be so. Do not think that I mean to deny you all pleasures, on the contrary I wish you all rational and gentlemanlike pleasures, and will always contribute all I can to them, but then they must not break in upon those necessary studys, that will be the ornaments of your youth, and the comfort of your old age. I was bred with all the indulgence possible, but was never allowed to go abroad till one o'Clok at Noon, and never suffered to lye out upon any account whatever. Think of all this, for you can think if you please. And God bless you.

To Mr Stanhope at Doctor
Dodd's house at Ealing in
Middlesex, by way of
London.

Free
Chesterfield

---

[85] Writing to his son (February 28, 1751), Chesterfield suggested that his writing, if received at the Secretary's office, would be sent to the decipherer; if by an antiquarian, he would "try it by the Runic, Celtic, or Sclavonian alphabet"; whereas a fine woman would think the *poulet* really came from the poulterer!

[86] Henry Frederick (1745–1790), younger brother of George III.

[87] Edwyn Stanhope (1729–1807) was first cousin to the boy's father. Six years previously, Chesterfield had written concerning him: "You must know that our kinsman has very strong and warm animal spirits, with a genius not quite so warm, and having nothing to do, is of course busy about trifles."—Letter to A. C. Stanhope, September 29, 1764.

[88] Near Newnham in Hampshire, some forty miles from London on the Winchester road (via Basingstoke).

[X]
[DICTATED][39]

Blackheath, 14 August 1772.

My dear Son,

I imagine you, at this moment, staring in the town of Leipzig, taking a liker[40] of the professors and they of you, but you will I hope see them with more attention than they will bestow upon you, for you must be conscious that between Dr Dodd's great negligence and your own idleness, you have lost, entirely, with regard to learning, the two best years of your life. You must now redeem them, especially with regard to the two studies which I have long recommended to you, natural law and the law of nations. Other things will come of course, such as riding, fencing, and dancing, the necessary ornaments of a gentleman, and I would not have you omit the perfect knowledge of the German tongue, which though not spoke universally in Europe, like French, has however its utility here in England. I am impatient to have your account of your reception and behaviour at Dresden, for the former will always depend upon the latter. I suppose Count Bruhl[41] and Mr Ernst['s] relations[42] have made all the ways smooth for you at that Court. I am acquainted there with one Count Einsedley,[43] who was a Minister in the late Elector's time, a man of sense and knowledge. If you mention me to him, I am sure he will show you all possible attention. Make my best compliments to M. Deyverdun. God bless you.

[signed] Chesterfield

A Monsieur [etc., as below, Letter XII]

[39] The dictated letters are normalized in spelling, capitalization, and punctuation; see the Introduction, pp. 14–15.

[40] Apparently "a try, attempt," recorded in the *English Dialect Dictionary* as current in Suffolk, but perhaps formerly more widely used, possibly as slang. I am indebted to Sir William A. Craigie, of the University of Chicago, for suggesting this as the most tenable explanation.

[41] Friedrich Aloys, Count Brühl (1739–1793), of Saxony, a man of the world and of letters, had spent some years in England; in 1767 he married the dowager Countess of Egremont, who in the following year bore him a son (*Gentleman's Magazine*, XXXVIII, 590; December, 1768).

[42] Ernst, Philip's intimate friend while they were both at Dr. Dodd's, had studied in Leipzig before the godson arrived there (see Chesterfield's two letters addressed to Ernst, January 25 and April 22, 1771); the only relative mentioned is an uncle, evidently the boy's guardian.

[43] Johann Georg Einsiedel (1730–1811), in 1763 Minister from Saxony to the Court of George III, but in the same year recalled to become a cabinet minister and Secretary of State.

[XI]
[DICTATED]

Blackheath, 20 August 1772.

My dear Son,

You are welcome to Leipzig, where your professor and you have began well, and I hope will continue so. He must know that it will be his interest to do so. I approve much of your *pension,* which is not the fourth part of what it would cost here, but I can not conceive why, in a German university, the German language should be prohibited under a penalty; in all events do you get a German master, for let people say what they will, it must be of use to you some time or other, and putting it at the worst, a language more than other people generally have is some advantage. At universities one must have to do with pedants, but if they are really learned pedants, they are a very useful part of society. There was a pedant overheard to thank God in his prayers for having made dictionary makers, and not without reason. What book of the laws of nations and nature does your professor think of giving you? I hope it is Puffendorf or Burlamachi," for Grotius sold his natural sentiments of liberty to make his court to Cardinal Richelieu when he was ambassador at Paris.

Did not you make a visit at Dresden, and if you did, what did you see there, or rather who? For persons are my great objects. Now that you are in a manner settled at Leipzig, I would have your *état* as considerable as anybody's there as to boarding, clothes, coach, &cra, &c., for I don't mind the expense, provided it is a proper one and not lavished away in idle fooleries, which you are too apt to do.

Pray have your teeth well kept, by the best operator at Leipzig, if there be any good one.

Tell M. Deyverdun that I am extremely his humble servant, and for you, God bless you.

[signed] Chesterfield

A Monsieur [etc., as elsewhere]

[Written on the third page of the foregoing:]
Sir,
You may depend upon my obeying your commands in respect to writing once a week. It is with the greatest satisfaction that I assure you that my Lord is infinitely better than he was when I had the honour to write you last, and I have the happiness to tell you that it is not upon my own authority that I give you this pleasing intelligence, but upon the authority of Dr Warren,[44] who is at this moment with his Lordship and who declares that he has no complaint but weaknes[s. I][46] wish I could tell you that my Lord was of the sa[me][47] opinion, but his Lordship has a thousand other complaints, though I can't help hoping that weakness is his only disorder.

My Lady torments me to death to know what is become of *Dragon*; for God['s] sake, Sir, say something about him in your next letter.

I have the honour to be, with the greatest respect, Sir,
Your most obedient
Humble servant,
J. Walsh[48]

---

[44] See below, p. 68, n. 93.

[45] Dr. Richard Warren (1731–1797), appointed physician to George III in 1762, and not only an eminent physician, but also an able manager of his business affairs, leaving an estate of more than £150,000.

[46] Manuscript torn.   [47] Manuscript torn.

[48] For an account of James Walsh, the *valet de chambre*, see the Introduction, p. 6.

[XII]
[DICTATED]

Blackheath, 3 September 1772.

My dear Son,

I received yesterday your letter of the 21st of August, and approve extremely of your intended plan of two or three little excursions, as well as of the present allotment of your time during your stay at Leipzig. In your private studies, pray take the English language into your consideration, in which I must tell you that you are very inaccurate, especially as to the grammatical part. The great regularity which by your account is observed in your hours I fear is too good to last; however, pray do you observe it strictly. Let others do what they will, in this point only I would have you be singular. Pray tell me, what are the places that you call the Gingétte's?[49] I know what the Gingéttes around Paris are, and these, I hope, are not like them. I like your privatessimums with the Professor Clodius;[50] be very careful and make the most of those two hours, for young as you are you have not too much time before you for the several duties of a man and a citizen. What is your present dress at Leipzig? Is it fine? Is it plain? I would have you conform in it to the general custom, but be rather above than below it. Are you grown since I saw you? I hope gentilier, however, for the worst models that you can form to yourself for your air and manner will be neither better nor worse than those you had taken here. I set Mr Rous against a professor, and Mr Thislethawit[51] against a young student at Göttingen. I would therefore not advise you to study any particular model, but to go on, as mere nature designed you, and wait for a proper model somewhere else. God bless you.

                        [signed] Chesterfield

A Monsieur
Monsieur Stanhope
Gentilhomme Anglois
    à
        Leipzig.
Paid

[Written on the second and third pages of the foregoing:]
Sir,
    Enclosed I send you a letter from Miss Stanhope,[52] which she desired might be forwarded to you. You have made Lady Chesterfield extremely happy to find that Dragon is not killed and eaten by the Blacks. But what I believe will be of more pleasure to hear, and which I assure you gives me great happiness to write, every letter my Lord receives from you gives more and more satisfaction to him, and I can assure you that your last letter gave his Lordship more real pleasure than he has felt of [sic] some time. His fondness for you seems to increase every day, and you can have no conception with what pleasure he hears you commended. I wish M. Deyverdun would write to him now and then; he was mightily pleased with his last letter. His Lordship['s] health is much better; I think that weakness seems to me to be his only disorder, but is by no means his only complaint, for that weakness is so excessive that it has depressed his spirits to such a degree that he will not bear to be told that he is any respect better.
    I paid to Messrs Drummonds yester[day][53] 1000 pounds, for which sum you will have credi[t with][54] Mr Benet according to your desire.
    I have the honour to be, with the truest respect,

            Sir,
                      Your most obedient
5 September   and very humble servant,
                                    J. Walsh

Miss Gee is married to-day.⁵⁵ Roberts is married to Mrs. Arnold. You saw by the papers that Walter Stanhope, Esq., is dead.⁵⁶ This letter should have gone the day before yesterday, but by a blunder was omitted.

---

⁴⁹ *Sic*, for *guinguettes*, taverns in the outskirts of a city.

⁵⁰ Christian August Clodius (1738–1784), best known as a poet; Professor of Philosophy at Leipzig for many years, and later of Logic, in 1782 he was called to be Professor of Poetry. His health broke down and he died two years later.

⁵¹ Who these gentlemen were does not appear, but in August, 1777, Philip Stanhope, now the fifth Earl of Chesterfield, married Anne, daughter of the Rev. Robert Thistlethwayte, D.D., of Norman Court and Southwick Park, Hants.

⁵² Presumably the boy's sister Margaret, frequently mentioned in Chesterfield's letters to A. C. Stanhope.

⁵³ Manuscript torn. ⁵⁴ Manuscript torn.

⁵⁵ According to the *Gentleman's Magazine* (XLII, 439), it was on September 6 that "Wm. White, Esq; of Old Bond street" married "Miss Gee of New Norfolk-street." The others named are still to be identified.

⁵⁶ Probably an error for Sir William Stanhope, who, old and without a legitimate son, was next in succession; with his death, the godson became the heir to the title.

[XIII]
[DICTATED]

Blackheath, 18 September 1772.

My dear Son,

You will judge of my disappointment when I tell you that I have received no letter from you of ten days, whereas in that time I had more reason to expect two than none. I want you to give me an account of your Leipzig life since your last, in which you touch upon it but lightly. Do you pursue your studies diligently, and is your professor satisfied with you? How go pleasures, for pleasures there must be? Are you acquainted with the principal ladies of Leipzig? Have you little parties of trifling play among them? I desire an account of your pleasures as much as I do of your studies; both are necessary for a gentleman. I don't ask how you and M. Deyverdun agree, because I rely upon the good sense of both to think it sure that you do. Do you grow more perfect in the German language? Are there coaches kept at Leipzig, and do you keep one, to carry you to and from Les Gingettes that you once mentioned?[57] Do you learn to dance, which is more material to a gentleman than fencing? However, I would have [you] know both, but do not rely upon the art of fencing, if you are ever unfortunate enough to be called out to single combat. If I were to indulge my impatience to know everything concerning you, I should never have done with my questions, but I must content myself with what information you are pleased to give me yourself or such as I can pick up by other means. God bless you.

[signed] C

A Monsieur [etc., as elsewhere]

---
[57] See Letter XII.

[XIV]
[DICTATED]

Blackheath, 29 September 1772.

My dear Son,

What can be become of you and M. Deyverdun? I have had a letter from neither, and this is the *third* I write to you. You remember that when you was a boy and here, I objected strongly to the perpetual motion of your fingers, but however, that was pardonable at your age, being more a boy at that age than any I ever knew; but now, you are old enough to know that the proper, and only proper, use of the fingers is writing. But as I am always inclined to justify you, I will lay my uneasiness upon the negligence of the post, and you will by your next let me know which it was. If it was study I enjoy that silence. If it was rational pleasure, I have no objection. But if it was idleness and sauntering about to buy things that you don't want, that is below a Man. Pray put an end to my doubts by the next post. And remember what I told you in London, that I am the only Stanhope in the world whose advice will be perfectly disinterested. The advice and professions of the male Stanhopes are calculated to govern you, when you come to have a vote in Parliament. Of the female Stanhopes, some Ready Money. So be upon your guard against them all. When you come to be at age, which will be when I am gone, you will have a difficult game to play; God direct you to play it well.

[signed] C

A Monsieur [etc., as elsewhere]

[XV]
[DICTATED]

London, 13 October 1772.

My dear Son,

I was very well pleased with the receipt of your last letter, supposing it to be a fair and true account of the employment of your time at Leipzig, but it is an old remark that travellers are not apt to observe the strictest veracity; but in the mean time I will take all you say for granted. How do you manage this Rebellion, as the newspapers call it? If you have taken a part, you will be a very young party man, indeed. But if you have, let it not be a violent part, such as our parties in England have long been divided into. Do you learn to dance, and is your dancing master, if you have one, as good a one as Dénoyer? I wish you could send me an attestation from M. Deyverdun of your proper behaviour, in every respect, at Leipzig. But I am afraid that he would make some difficulty with regard to such an affidavit. All the Stanhopes here are, or pretend to be, your humble servants, but you know that I have already given you some salutary cautions upon that head; and so, God bless you.

[signed] C

A Monsieur [etc., as elsewhere]

[Written on the third page of the foregoing:]
Sir,

My Lord has had a pretty severe return of his purging attended by a fever, which a good deal alarmed the doctor. It has, however, I thank God, gone off, and at this time his Lordship is, except his weakness, tolerably well.

I have the honour to be, with the greatest respect,

Sir, Your most obedient Humble servant,
J. Walsh.

[XVI]
[DICTATED]

Chesterfield House, 29 October 1772.

My dear Son,

You see I don't stand upon ceremony with you, for you are a letter or two in my debt, but where you are nearly concerned I don't mind that. This is the case now. And I [ca]n⁸⁸ not help congratulating you upon your late [loss] of fourscore pounds at quinze. For if you had w[on] as much, it would have given you a taste f[or g]aming, as it did me the first time I played, whereas if I had lost as much, it would I dare say have disgusted me of play. But go on, and by that time that I die, you will have made a pretty little fortune of your own, and not want anything that I may happen to leave you. M. Deyverdun will I dare say be of my opinion. Pray write me word if he is so or not, for he is a man of sense.

What are you doing now, at the good University of Leipzig? Are you making yourself master of the German language? The law of nature and the law of nations? Or sauntering about the Fair, and buying whatever you don't want?

Now I will give you a little news from hence. Doctor and Mrs Dodd have been at Margate to refresh themselves, and from thence took a trip, as [the]y call it, to Paris, to the great improvemen[t] of Mrs Dodd's air and manners. They staid v[ery] little while there, and are come back just as [the]y went. These trips you know in your little experience to be very expensive. Where the money is found, God knows. I recommend to you most earnestly to consider how little time you have to lose. You are very backward in all useful learning. May your endeavours to retrieve time lost be successful. God bless you.

A Monsieur [signed] C
Monsieur Stanhope
Gentilhomme Anglois
    à
        Leipzig.
Paid

---

[89] This letter is torn in two places, affecting several words.

[XVII]
[DICTATED]

Chesterfield House, 20 November 1772.

My dear Son,

I will no more accuse you of negligence, when I have now three letters of yours lying before me, but we will come to the point. I presume you wrote the French letter to show me that you had not forgot your French, but unfortunately it did not answer that purpose; on the contrary, it is very bad French, and I desire that you will apply yourself to be correct and even elegant in that necessary language, for none of the great affairs of Europe are transacted in any other, and he who is the most master of the language in which he negociates will always be too hard for him who is not so perfect in it. Your English wants a great deal of being either correct or elegant, and you never should have that out of your thoughts. By your account you have passed your time as I could have wished lately. I wish I could have seen you at dinner with the Elector of Saxony, where I hope you did not behave in that slouching negligent manner which you did too often here. I am glad that you are returned to Leipzig, where M. Clodius's closet will be for some time properer for you than the drawing rooms.

When you happen to see Mr Osborne again make him many compliments from me, for his great civility to you. As also to M. Deyverdun. God bless you.

[signed] C

A Monsieur [etc., as elsewhere]

[Written on the third page of the foregoing:]

Sir,

I received your commands, and you may depend upon my calling at Egremont House,[59] about the time you mention. My Lord, Sir, I think continues much the same as when you left him; if there is any alteration, it is certainly for the better. I mean in his Lordship's health, for his weakness is as bad as ever.

By this day's post I have the honour to s[end a][60] letter which you ought to have had sent you m[any][61] weeks ago, but it was sent to my Lord out of [sic; in] the coun[tr]y.[62] His Lordship left it on his table and forgot it.

I have the honour to be with the greatest respect,

Sir,
Your most devoted
Humble servant,
J. Walsh.

---

[59] In Piccadilly. The occasion was presumably the coming of age on December 18 of the third Earl, Sir George O'Brien Wyndham (1751–1837). Count Brühl was his stepfather (see above, p. 34 and n. 41).

[60] Manuscript torn.   [61] Manuscript torn.   [62] Manuscript torn.

[XVIII]
[DICTATED]

Chesterfield House, 23 November 1772.

My dear Son,

This letter is not to pay an epistolary debt, but to contract one from you. If you knew how interesting every letter from you is to me, you would rather be in advance than in debt to me. The town is going to begin now, as the Parliament will sit on Thursday, where as yet you have nothing to do, but where in four years' time I hope you will be advantageously heard of. At least, I am persuaded that my existence will be no hindrance to it.

To give you now a little domestic trash, I will tell you that Dr Dodd has set up a new chariot, too showish for a parson, and too expensive for a bankrupt, as I take the poor man now to be. I have not seen him, since you went, but once, but I have had several messages from him, all which seem to be the effects of necessity, and that he will not lose the little hold that he has upon me, when he is quite sinking. I can never write to you without inculcating most strongly your application to your serious studies, for which, I must tell you again and again, you have left but little time. Mend, mend, and God bless you.

[signed] C

A Monsieur
Monsieur Stanhope
Gentilhomme Anglois
  à
   Leipzig.
Paid

[XIX]
[DICTATED]

Chesterfield House, 22 December 1772.

My dear Son,

I am in your debt four letters, and this letter would have been a very voluminous one, in answer to the various matters contained in it [*sic*; them], if my health would have permitted it. But the latter end of last week I was not only within three days, but in my mind within three hours of giving all up to you, which for your sake only I should have been sorry for. I am now so far recovered as possibly to last as long as a very advanced old age will allow. More or less, is equal to me, except upon your account. A letter to you from Dr Dodd will show you the utmost art that either man or woman can exert to keep a hold upon you. You will have several of these arts employed upon you; all your acquaintances will try their utmost skill to strip and govern you, but this letter of Dr Dodd's is in my opinion the utmost effort of human cunning. Mrs Dodd is gently justified in it, with regard to you. The Doctor, it seems, always loved you, and loves you still, but will love you a great deal better when you shall be in possession of your title and estate, and the event, which he thinks and with reason, can not be very remote.

I have received very safe and in very good condition your dejeunée, which is not only extremely fine, but very pretty. I am afraid you laid out too much money for me, in so splendid a bauble, but when I consider that all your present baubles will be your future ornaments, I will not grudge them.

God bless you. When I am better able you shall hear a great deal further from me.

[signed] C

A Monsieur [etc., as elsewhere]

[Written separately, but of the same date as the foregoing:]
Chesterfield House, 22 December 1772.
Sir,
Enclosed I send you a letter sent me by Dr Dodd, desiring me to direct it and send it to you. My Lord, however, thought proper to order me to break the seal and read it to him. By the letter which his Lordship sends you by this post, you will receive his thoughts upon its contents. You will also receive a letter by this post from Miss Stanhope, which my Lord did not break open. I could have wished that he had not seen the one I sent you from her about ten days ago, for though I can't say he was angry, yet your not having paid for the china before you left England made him think you had not dealt fairly with him, by not telling him of all your debts. If you should for the future have occasion for any money to be paid in any part of England, you may draw upon me for it, and repay me either by draft upon Mr Hewit, or any other way that may be more agreeable to you. But you will please to remember that if I have the honour to be your banker, the drafts must be in proportion to the bank, which I fear will seldom be able to answer a draft of above twenty or thirty pounds at once. I paid last Tuesday into Messrs Drummonds' hands one thousand pounds, for which you will have credit at Leipzig. This makes three thousand two hundred pounds since your departure from hence. Everybody admires your taste, in the dejeunée you have sent my Lord, but what I am sure is of the most consequence to you, I have the pleasure to assure you that my Lord is much pleased at your having sent it him.

I confess honestly, Sir, that I was much afraid that this letter would have been addressed to you in a different title, your amiable father[63] having within these ten days had, I think, the most severe struggle that ever man got the better of. Weak and debilitated as he was, by near a twelvemonth's illness, at his age, consider what it must be to be seized with a flux that would occasion thirteen or fourteen stools a day, bouncing from him without the least notice, or the power of retention. Add to this a total loss of appetite and sleep, attended at the same time with so violent a fever as to occasion a delirium with very few intervals. Consider, I say, Sir, how many chances there must be against a recovery from so very deplorable a situation! And yet I have the happiness to inform you that his Lordship has weathered this storm. And that there is all the reason to hope that he will in a few days be as well (at least) as he has been for some time before it happened.

His Lordship has this moment received a le[tter][64] from you dated the 12th inst., with which he is mu[ch][65] pleased, as soon as I had read it to him. He said, "[That][66] is the best letter I ever received from the Boy," and with much pleasure showed it to my Lady, who did not so much approve of it, because *Dragon* was not mentioned in it.

Mr L. Stanhope,[67] who was almost constantly here while my Lord was so very ill, and was indeed the only person he would speak to, is now gone for the holidays to the Duke of Chandos's.[68] May I beg you to present my humble respect to M. Deyverdun?

    I am,
        Sir, with the greatest respect,
            Your most obedient humble servant,

                              J. Walsh.

A Monsieur [etc., as elsewhere]

---

[63] *I.e.*, godfather, the Earl; Mr. A. C. Stanhope, the boy's father, had died in 1770.

[64] Manuscript torn.   [65] Manuscript torn.   [66] Manuscript torn.

[67] Lovell Stanhope (d. 1783), the youngest brother of A. C. Stanhope, was one of the executors of Chesterfield's will.

[68] James Brydges (1731–1789), the third Duke. When Canons, the first Duke's great house, was torn down and sold for its materials, the staircase went into Chesterfield House.

[XX]
[DICTATED]

Chesterfield House, 8 January 1773.

My dear Son,

I have received yours of the 25th past by which you tell me that you intended to set out soon for Berlin. I am very curious to know your reception at that Court, which I believe will be a very good one, as accidents have fortunately thrown it in my way to please that great Prince.⁶⁹ But when I have said this, I must tell you that it is what you have done that I am curious always to know, and not what you intend to do. I am not solicitous to know where you intend to go, as I presume those motions are entirely directed by M. Deyverdun; at least, I am sure they ought to be so. Tell me in your next how you and M. Clodius go on. As good friends, I hope, for then his instructions will be the more acceptable, as the instructions of friends will always make a deeper and more lasting impression than of Master and Scholar.

I find by your letter that you suppose me at Bath, as usual at this time of the year, but my complaints were of a quite different nature from those which hitherto have sent me there. I have had a lurking fever these eight months, which has taken away the use of my legs and made me the wretched cripple that I am now. I reflect how much worse I should have been now, if I had lived like other young people of my time in town.⁷⁰ I hope the custom of what the Bears here call sober drinking is not got to Leipzig, for I have observed that sober drinking consists in being neither drunk or sober at night, which is the silliest situation that a man can be in. God bless you.

A Monsieur [signed] C
Monsieur Stanhope
Gentilhomme Anglois
    à
        Leipzig.
Paid

---

[69] Frederick the Great, for whom Chesterfield frequently expressed the highest admiration. See the next letter; also that to Voltaire, August 27, 1752 (Dobrée, V, 1927).

[70] Yet he had written his son (April 25, 1758): "Neither my memory nor my invention are now what they formerly were. It is in great measure my own fault; I cannot accuse Nature, for I abused her, and it is reasonable I should suffer for it." None the less, he may easily have stopped far short of many of his companions; cf. among others the letters of March 27, 1747, and December 26, 1749.

[XXI]
[DICTATED]

Chesterfield House, 22 January 1773.

My dear Son,

I received in due time your letter of the 3d inst. and by the same post was favored with one from M. Deyverdun, which gave me, [with] great submission to you, perhaps more pleasure than yours, for his testimony as far as it goes is unsuspected of partiality and he clears you of the three shining vices of youth at your age: neither drinking, gaming, nor women seem to have tainted your character. These I own are negative virtues, and there is one qualification wanting, and which is as necessary for a gentleman as any one that I know. I mean, application to your studies, for ignorance will disgrace you, in spite of any good qualities that you may have. Therefore I earnestly beg of you, my dear son, to be diligent and to mind your lectures with M. Clodius and others. Consider what a figure you must make in the world, if you are ignorant of the rights and privileges of yourself and your fellow creatures. Make my best compliments to M. Deyverdun, whose verses[n] everybody must approve; I am sure I do. I want extremely to hear the particulars of your reception at Berlin which, if the King of Prussia continues in the same mind that he was in some months ago, will be a very gracious one, and I shall almost envy you those moments which you will pass with the greatest man in the world. Never man possessed all the advantages of nature and

---

[n] Deyverdun wrote several works, but I have found no other mention of his verses.

education that His Majesty does. I would willingly compound for your having a fourth part of them.

God bless you.

[signed] C

A Monsieur
Monsieur Stanhope
Gentilhomme Anglois
    à
       Leipzig.
Paid

[XXII]
[DICTATED]

Chesterfield House, 31 January 1773.

My dear Son,

I received by the last post your letter of the 11th inst. wrote in French, I suppose to show me that you have not neglected that necessary language since you have left England, but instead of that you have showed me by the badness of your French that you have never thought of it since. Was *plus bonne* ever thought of for the comparatif when *meillieur* was so near at hand? How that expression would have made a French company laugh, I leave to you to consider. I never doubted of the good reception that you would meet with at Berlin, but I must say that you did not deserve it. Did ever anybody give the epithet you give in your letter to a Crowned Head or Sovereign Prince? When you have a little more experience of the world you will know that all letters are opened, read, and folded up again as well as they were at first. Sovereigns have long arms and piercing eyes, and can see and do what common persons can not; therefore pray be more guarded for the future in what you say of those Great Persons. It is very possible that if that Great Person saw by inspection of your letter the epithet you give him, he might have sent you for a time to his castle of Spondau.ⁿ However, a few years older and a good deal of experience, which you may have in that time, will set all these matters right.

Make my compliments to M. Deyverdun and desire him from me to animate and spur you up to attention, which I almost despair of his being able to do, and without which, let me tell you, you will be Nobody. Which after my attention to your improvement would be most disgraceful to you. In the mean time God bless you.

A Monsieur   [signed] C
Monsieur Stanhope
Gentilhomme Anglois
    à
        Leipzig.
Paid

---

[73] *I.e.*, Spandau, near Berlin.

[XXIII]
[DICTATED]

Chesterfield House, 9 February 1773.

My dear Son,

I like your accounts from Berlin, by which it appears that you see what you do see and that you hear what you do hear, which a great many people do not do. And if accounts are not correct, they only serve to mislead instead of informing. I hope this letter will find M. Clodius and you tête-à-tête studying Grotius, Puffendorf, or Burlamachi, who for the law of nations is in my opinion worth the other two.

I have had the pleasure of hearing good accounts of you from two different quarters, that is, as to your manners and politeness, for without them you are and will be *Nobody*. At Berlin, I find, all was done that was possible to amuse you, from His Majesty down to the last of the courtiers, for which, without vanity, I look upon myself to be particularly obliged to him.

Yesterday Lady Stanhope was married to a Captain Morris,[73] whose whole fortune consists in his bodily strength and activity; however, you have no reason to fear a pretender to your crown and dignity, for whatever comes from this match the Captain must take care of.

Whenever you write to me, write more an account of yourself than of the things you have seen; send me word what happens to you, in love, or politics, or gazing. God bless you.

[signed] C

A Monsieur [etc., as elsewhere]

---

[73] She was the widow of Sir William; the Captain was Charles Morris (1745–1838), a song-writer and *bon vivant*.

[XXIV]
[DICTATED]

Chesterfield House, 19 February 1773.

My dear Son,

The music you sent for will get to you as soon as possible, but it is because you say it is for a lady, for you know that when we parted you promised me never to turn piper or fiddler. I do not know by what strange luck music has got the name of one of the liberal arts. I don't see what can entitle it to that distinction, and for my part, I declare that I would rather be reckoned the best barber than the best fiddler in England. Nothing degrades a gentleman more than performing upon any instrument whatever. It brings him into ill company and makes him proud of his shame, by courting the favour of Signior de Geordino,[74] as the Duke of Ancaster[75] experienced five or six years ago. He had done my Lord Duke the honour of passing the summer at His Grace's house in the country, and when the jackanapes went away, he gave among the servants all the money the Duke had given him. In short, those Italian virtuosi are allowed to be the scum of the whole earth. Keep from their acquaintance. A glaring example how pernicious an intimacy is with those jackanapeses may be seen in the Duke of Devonshire,[76] who p[a]sses[77] most of his evenings with only Signior de Geordino and Signior Bach.[78]

Are you restored to your state of tranquillity at Leipzig? I hope you are, for upon my word, you have no time to lose. As to the studies you were about when you left Leipzig, they are necessary, they are pleasing. And I don't know that anything that was called pleasing was so agree-

60 LETTERS OF LORD CHESTERFIELD

able to me as the laws of nature and nations. God bless you.
My compliments to M. Deyverdun.

[signed] C

A Monsieur
Monsieur Stanhope
Gentilhomme Anglois
    à
        Leipzig.
Paid

[Written on the third page of the foregoing:]

Sir,

According to your orders, I have bought the music, and shall take care to send it directed to you at Leipzig by the first Hambro[79] ship that sails, with orders to the captain to forward it to you as directed. The expense is 1L. 10s. 3d. as you will see by the bill and receipt that accompanies it. Any further commands that you may please to honour me with, I shall with great[80] pleasure obey.

My Lord is, I thank God, tolerably well in his health, but still continues in point of weakness much as when you left him.

I have the honour to be, with the greatest respect,

Sir,
Your most dutiful
Servant,
J. Walsh.

---

[74] With his father and two sisters, Tommaso Giordani (*ca.* 1733–1806) came to London about 1753; his younger brother followed in 1772. Both were composers. Tommaso, in the '60's and later, was much in Dublin.

[75] Peregrine, third Duke (1714–1778).

[76] William Cavendish, fifth Duke (1748–1811).   [77] Manuscript torn.

[78] Probably Johann Christian Bach (1735–1782), youngest son of the great Johann Sebastian Bach, and himself a composer of some note. He lived in London from 1762 until his death.

[79] Hamburg.

[80] The bottom part of this word is torn away.

[XXV]
[DICTATED]

Chesterfield House, 7 March 1773.

My dear Son,

When I do anything for my own momentary satisfaction, I first consider whether it will give you a lasting one or not, for my span is short, whereas yours may be very long if you manage it well. I have lately bought a very fine picture of Claude Lorrain,[81] which though it cost me [a][82] great deal of money you will I hope not disapprove of. These things are called heirlooms in a family, of which I have made many that are not to be sold or squandered away by idle young fellows, but are to remain in a family together with the title and the estate. I therefore recommend to you to have all the heirlooms I shall leave kept sacred.[83] To tell you the truth, I suspect you extremely upon the article of economy; since you have been abroad, you have drawn upon me like a horse, without assigning any particular reason for it, such as your expeditions to Dresden and Berlin. This day I pay to Messrs Drummond on your account a thousand pounds, which makes four thousand two hundred pounds that I have paid them on your account since your departure from hence, which you know was only last June.[84] I hope I shall hear no more of these demands for some time. I am very far from being inclined to stint you, but at the same time, know that I should be blamed for giving to any young traveller such a profusion of money. I recommend to you only a decent frugality, which will enable you to make a better figure abroad than an idle dissipation of your allowance will do.

God bless you.

[signed] C[85]

A Monsieur [etc., as elsewhere]

[Written on the third page of the foregoing:]
Sir,

It gives me great pain that I can not give you a more agreeable account of my Lord's health than the following. After having been pretty near in the same situation as when you left him, till within this fortnight, when there was hopes of his getting a little stro[nger, his][86] legs all at once began to sw[ell and have been in]creasing[87] ever since, but within [?three][88] days to a most alarming degree, and what is much worse, the swelling is not confined to the legs but has got up into his body, a circumstance which gives Doctor Warren[89] great uneasiness. Should there be any material change between this day and next post day, I shall certainly inform you of it. I pray God that it may be for the better.

I have the honour to be,

Sir, Your most obedient Humble servant,

J. Walsh.

---

[81] "My Lord Chesterfield bought a Claude the other day for four hundred guineas, and a Madame de la Vallière for four. He said, 'Well! if I am laughed at for giving so much for a landscape, at least it must be allowed that I have my women cheap.' Is not it charming to be so agreeable quite to the door of one's coffin?"—Walpole to the Countess of Upper Ossory, March 11, 1773.

[82] Manuscript torn.

[83] Chesterfield had already taken legal precautions in this regard: by his will not only were the "household goods, plate, statues, bustoes, vases, books, pictures, and furniture" entailed with the estate, but also "the large brilliant diamond ring which I commonly wear myself and which was left me by the late Dutchess of Marlborough"; after leaving a rose diamond ring to his sister, Lady Gertrude Hotham, he proceeded, "I give unto my said wife the use of the rest of her and my jewels for her life and after her decease I give the use of the said jewels unto my said godson Philip Stanhope for his life, and after his decease I give the use of the said jewels to such person as shall for the time being be Earl of Chesterfield, it being my will that the said jewels shall always descend and go as heirlooms with the title of Earl of Chesterfield as far as law or equity will permit."

[84] By an odd coincidence, £4200 was the sum specified in Dr. Dodd's forged draft!

[85] Seventeen days later, Chesterfield died (March 24, 1773).

[86] MS torn. [87] MS torn. [88] MS torn. [89] See above, p. 37, n. 45.

[XXVI]

A Monsieur D'ayverdun.⁹⁰

Cette Lettre est le dernier effort d'une main tremblante,⁹¹ et d'un esprit baissé par l'age et les maladies. Ie confie a vos soins Monsieur L'education ulterieure d'un enfant qui m'est Cher tant par la Justesse de son esprit, que par les qualitez de son cœur, et Je suis persuadé que vous ne trouverez pas mauvais, que Je vous explique en gros le plan, que Ie souhaitte que vous suiviez pour mettre la derniere main a son Education qui Jusqu'a present n'a pas été negligee.⁹²

Ie l'envoye d'abord a Leipsig ou Je voudrois qu'il restat une annee entiere, non seulement pour le perfectionner dans L'etude des belles lettres, mais pour lui enseigner le droit naturel, et le droit des gens, le premier par l'excellent livre de Burlamachi,⁹³ le dernier par Puffendorf plutot que par Grotius qui par une lache complaisance pour le Cardinal de Richelieu, etablit le pouvoir absolu des Roix, et L'esclavage des peuples; sentimens que le sens commun, l'oblige de démentir dans la suitte de son livre. Pendant son sejour a Leipsig, Ie voudrois qu'il fut logé et nourri dans la maison du plus habile Professeur des Belles Lettres où il apprendroit peutétre plus par la conversation Iournaliere du Professeur, que par ses leçons dans les formes. Ie ne voudrois nullement qu'il tint son petit menage chez lui, dont la suitte necessaire seroit qu'il prieroit les Anglois (si malheureusent⁹⁴ il y en auroit a Leipsig) qui viendroient volontiers s'enyvrer *Moult tristement* chez lui *a la mode de leur païs*.⁹⁵ Au reste Monsieur ne croyez pas que Ie dis çeçy a cause de quelques Rixthalers que cela me couteroit, rien moins car au contraire Ie veux qu'il fasse une aussi belle depense en Equipage et en habits, que qui que ce soit à Leipsig, fut-ce meme un *Serenissime*. L'avantage que Je me propose en lui faisant manger a une espece de Table d'Hôte, c'est de lui faire voir toutte sort de Caracteres et de Mœurs, car Je [*interl.:* ne] l'envoye pas voiager, pour voir des Choses mais pour voir des personnes de toutte sorte, et J'aimerois mieux qu'il vit le moindre des Conseillers de l'Electeur Palatin que la grosse Tonne d'Heidleberg.⁹⁶

Pour les exercices, cela s'en va sans dire, a l'exception seulement de la danse, que peutetre il vaudroit mieux qu'il n'apprit pas durant son sejour a Leipsig, Car J'avoue que Ie n'ay pas d'Idees des graces qu'un Maitre a dansér de la confession d'Augsbourg lui pouroit donner. Venons aux Mœurs. Pour le jeu et la boisson, il faut faire l'impossible pour les corriger absolument, montréz lui la bassesse degradante de ces deux Vices, et si vos representations ne font poit⁹⁷ d'effet, il faut en informer ceux a qui il tient de plus pres dans ce pais icy. Par rapport aux femmes ce n'est pas la mene⁹⁸ chose. Il seroit Chimerique d'Esperer qu'un Jeune Drole plein de Santé et de Vigueur conservat la Chasteté. Mais tout ce que vous pouvez et devez faire est d'empecher que cette debauche, ne soit honteuse et deshonorante, et n'interresse sa santé. S'il sagit de la servante, ou de la Maitresse de la Maison, Il me semble que vous ferez bien de l[']ignorer. S'il est question d'une Amourette avec quelque femme de condition et du bon ton, I'avoue que Ie ne l'interromperois pas, puis que rien ne degraisse tant⁹⁹ un Jeune homme qu'un arrangement avec une femme de condition dans la bonne compagnie.¹⁰⁰

Par rapport aux *manieres* il est absolument necessaire pour lui de les avoir tres douces et polies, Il en a deja quelques Idees, et il sent bien la necessité de plaire, mais pour les moyens il n'y a qu'un grand usage du monde et de la bonne compagnie qui puisse les lui enseigner. Ie vous supplie donc Monsieur, ayez une attention toutte particuliere a cet article si necessaire pour lui, et que vous possédez si bien vous même. Par sa naissance il doit necessairement etre dans la Chambre haute, et meme bien tôt, où J'espere et Je crois meme qu'il pourra briller par son sçavoir et ses talens naturels, mais Ie ne voudrois pas pour chose au monde qu'il fut simplement un *gros Milord d'Angleterre,* au contraire Je souhaitterois ardemment qu'il brillat a la Cour egalement par ses Manieres douces et polies, Enfin, qu'il fut ce qu'on appelle en Francois un parfaittement honnête et galant Homme, et en Anglois a *Gentleman*[.][101]

Quand il aura fini son annee a Leipsig, Ie voudrois, qu'il employât six mois a se decrotter, dans les endroits les moins infestez par ses compatriotes. Ils fourmillent toujours a Geneve et a Lausanne, Nancy, Luneville, Lisle, ou Dijon en Bourgogne, seroient ils des lieux de Sureté? Vous scaurez cela mieux que moy, et Je suis sur que vous en profiterez, autant que vous pourrez.

Apres ces dixhuit Mois finis, il faut venir a Paris, le lieu le plus dangereux, mais en meme tems le plus necessaire, où il puisse faire quelque sejour. Tant d'Anglois debauchez d'un coté, tant de Calypsos de l'autre! Il faut s[']en remettre a la providence, a son propre bon sens, et a vos conseils, qui pourront faire quelque chose mais pas be[a]ucoup. A Paris il ne peut pas manger a Table d'Hôte. Il faut qu'il mange chez lui quand il n'est pas [*interl.:* invité] ailleurs. Qu'il y soit tres bien logé, et que son Equipage et ses habits soient des plus propres. Qu'il apprenne chez lui du Maitre a danser le plus a la mode, et qu'il aprenne ses autres exercices comme de monter à[102] Cheval et de faire des armes, a L'Academie la plus frequentee par la Jeune Noblesse francoise.[103] Je voudrois qu'il restat au moins une annee entière a Paris pour se naturaliser en quelque sorte François. Apres cela il peut allér dans les parties Meridionales de la France, pour voir seulement Montpelier, Bourdeaux Toulouse et Aix en Provence Lyons &ra ce qui prendra peu de tems. Qu'il voye aussi çeux des Cantons Suisses qui meritent le plus son attention. Ayant expedié tout cela, Ie veux qu'il aille aux plus celebres Cours d'Allemagne, pas pour en voir simplement les batimens, mais pour connoitre les Souverains, les Ministres, les mœurs et les manieres. Comme par exemple il devroit rester a la Cour de Vienne quatre mois, autant a la Cour de Berlin. Un a Munich, un a Manheim, un a Dresde. Pour les petits Serenissimes de L'allemagne Il na qu'a [sic] les prendre dans son Chemin et [? canc.: leur] leur faire la Reverence en passant. En passant par la Flandrqui [sic] merite bien d'etre vue, Il devroit [canc.: au moins] faire un sejour de cinq mois a la Haye, pour apprendre a fond la forme de ce gouvernement compliqué, et pour y connoitre les Ministres de touttes les Cours de [canc.: touttes les Cours] de L'Europe. Son Nom ne lui nuira pas en Hollande.[104]

Vous serez sans doute surpris Monsieur que Ie [interl.: ne] nomme pas seulement L'Italie; la raison en est, que Je [interl.: ne] veux pas qu'il y aille du tout. C'est a present le siege de L'Atheisme, de la Sodomee, et des mauvaises Manieres. Les exemples des Jeunes Anglois qui en reviennent, et aussi de ceux qui n'en reviennent pas, comme Milord Tilney,[105] Milord Cowper[106] &ra m'effrayent trop; ceux qui en echappent les moins gâtez en reviennent des frivoles Joueurs du Clavecin ou du Violon ou bien des ignorants Virtuosi[.] Il est vray qu'il y a des restes tres respectables de la belle antiquité, Mais en meme tems ce ne sont que des choses et comme Je ne le fais pas voiager pour voir des Choses mais des personnes, et surement ce ne sera pas les Italiens.

Si apres avoir bien vu les païs susmentionnez vous pouvez lui persuader de faire le tour du nord I'en seray bien aise; Ie veux dire Petersbourg, Stockholm et Copenhague, avec lesquels L'Angleterre aura toujours plus ou moins a faire. Sept ou huit mois suffiront pour cette tournée, car Je ne demande pas qu'il voye ces pais, mais seulement ces Cours. Il sera bientôt d'un rang et il aura un bien, qui le mettront a meme de faire valoir Son Talent, et Je crois qu'il en a assez pour se distinguér dans le monde. Mais il faut que ses voiages soient dirigés a cet objet preferablement a tout autre.[107]

Il n'y a que l'usage du grande monde et de la bonne compagnie qui puisse polir un Jeune homme, I'entends egalement la compagnie des femmes, comme des hommes; Et c'est de ce coté la qu'il manque le plus, comme tous les Anglois.[108] C'est pourquoy Ie vous supplie Monsieur d'avoir une attention toutte particuliere a cet objet Capital. poussez le dans le beau monde, faittes lui prendre le ton de la bonne compagnie, fut-ce meme au depens de sa Chasteté.

Apres avoir quitté Leipsig il pourra depenser quinze cent livres Sterlin par an, et en cas de besoin, nous ne nous brouillerons pas pour quelques centaines de pieces de plus.[109]

Vous signerez tous deux ses lettres de change sur votre Banquier a Londres, pour eviter toutte pierre d'achopement.

Vous sentez bien Monsieur que dans ses voiages, et surtout en Allemagne, un homme que n'a pas le plus beau des Chateaux possibles, et qui ne peut pas prouver ses trente deux quartiers comme le Baron de Tonder ter Tronk,[110] n'est point admissible aux Tables des Grands Seigneurs, c'est pourquoy il faut le laisser aller seul sur sa bonne foy.

A present que Ie vous ay suffisament expliqué mes sentimens touchant mon Jeune Garçon, Ie finis cette lettre deja trop longue, sans complimens, vous ayant donné des preuves indubitables de mon esteme et de ma confiance avec lesquels Ie suis parfaittem^t
Monsieur
      Votre tres humb^{le} serviteur
        Chesterfield
A Blackheath, ce 26 Juillet
  1771

[This letter was provided with a separate envelope, inscribed:] This to be given to Monsieur D'ayverdun. In case I should dye before he returns, and before he goes abroad with my Godson.

---

[90] For Georges Deyverdun, see the Introduction, pp. 8–9.

To Professor Harcourt Brown, Chairman of the Department of Romance Languages at Brown University, I am indebted for suggestions in the transcription and translation of this letter.

[91] This is almost the last letter in Chesterfield's own hand; the "posthumous letter," left to be given the godson after Chesterfield's death, was written earlier.

[92] At this point, as repeatedly below, the pen (or the ink or both) changes, indicating that the letter was written over a long period of time.

[93] Jean-Jacques Burlamaqui (1694–1748), of Geneva, built on Grotius, Puffendorf, and Barbeyrac, their commentator, but arrived at his own conclusions. According to the *Nouvelle Biographie Générale*, his method was almost that of geometry applied to society!

Baron Samuel von Puffendorf (1631–1694) had been one of the authors recommended to the illegitimate son.

Hugo Grotius (in Dutch, Huig van Groot; 1583–1645) began to write his *De jure belli et pacis* in 1623, publishing it in 1625, in Paris. Richelieu became Prime Minister in 1624. When Grotius became ambassador at Paris (1635), he seems to have been for the most part working against Richelieu.

⁹⁴ *Sic* in MS.

⁹⁵ Writing to Madame de Monconseil, February 14, 1763, Chesterfield attributed this phrase to Froissart; in *The World*, no. 92 (October 3, 1754), he had given a fuller quotation: "Ils se saoulerent grandement, et se divertirent moult tristement à la mode de leur païs."

⁹⁶ In 1751 the third tun, of 49,000 gallons capacity, was built in the castle cellar at Heidelberg.

A second change in the pen occurs here.

⁹⁷ *Sic;* point. ⁹⁸ *Sic;* même.

⁹⁹ The word *tant* was added in the margin, *un* beginning a new line; the penmanship is that of the following paragraph.

¹⁰⁰ A third change in the pen occurs here.

¹⁰¹ A fourth change in the pen occurs here.

¹⁰² Written over *le*.

¹⁰³ A fifth change in the pen occurs here; the sentences from here to the end of the paragraph are written with the least legibility of any in this letter, and apparently with great difficulty.

¹⁰⁴ Chesterfield looked back with pride to his two embassies there, many years earlier.

A sixth change in the pen occurs here.

¹⁰⁵ Apparently John Tilney (1712–1784), the second Earl. Lord Bruce saw a Lord Tilney in Italy (August 8, 1753; see the Historical MSS Commission, *MSS of the Earl of Charlemont*, p. 186); however, Walpole visited the second Earl in England two years later (letter to Richard Bentley, July 17, 1755).

¹⁰⁶ George Nassau Cowper, concerning whom Walpole repeatedly made remarks in his letters. Walpole's own footnote to his letter to Sir Horace Mann (November 13, 1765, the portion added November 15) is illuminating: "The third Earl of Cowper, who had gone to travel in his father's life, fell in love with a married lady, and could not be prevailed on by the most earnest entreaties of his dying father to come to England. He continued there [in Italy] for many years after the death of his father and the extinction of his own passion: married an English young gentlewoman there, and in the year 1781 sent his children by her to England without coming himself." In 1786, however, he did finally visit England, where Walpole met him.

¹⁰⁷ A seventh change in the pen occurs here.

¹⁰⁸ An eighth (and last) change in the pen occurs here.

¹⁰⁹ But in the first nine months, while still at Leipzig, the boy drew on the Earl for £4200. See Letter XXV.

¹¹⁰ The chateaux, the quarters, and the Baron of Thunder-ten-tronckh all appear in the first chapter of *Candide*.

Translation

[Where Chesterfield's own phrases in the various earlier plans can be used without violating the sense, they appear enclosed in angles, thus: < >; see the Introduction, page 11.]

This letter is the final effort of a trembling hand, and of a spirit reduced by age and disease. I confide to your care, Monsieur, the further education of a youth who is dear to me as much for the strength of his mind as for the qualities of his heart; and I am persuaded that you will not take it amiss that I should explain in general the plan which I wish you to follow in order to put the last touch to his education, which has so far not been neglected.

I am sending him first to Leipzig, where I should like him to remain a whole year, not only to perfect him in the study of the belles-lettres, but to teach him <the law of nature and of nations,> the former by Burlamaqui's excellent book, the latter in Puffendorf rather than in Grotius, who through a weak complaisance for the Cardinal de Richelieu established <the absolute power of Kings> and the slavery of peoples—sentiments which <common sense obliges him to contradict in the sequel of his book.> During his stay at Leipzig, <I would have him lodged and boarded in the house of> the most skilled *Professeur des belles-lettres*, where he would perhaps acquire more by the daily conversation of the teacher than by his formal lessons. I should by no means wish that he maintain his establishment in his own quarters, of which the necessary consequence would be that he would ask in the English (if unhappily there should be any of them at Leipzig), who would willingly come to get drunk with him, *full sadly after the fashion of their country*. However, Monsieur, do not think that I say this for the sake of a few rix-dollars which it would cost me; nothing less, for on the contrary I wish him to make as seemly an outlay in equipage and livery as anyone in Leipzig, were he even a *Sérénissime*. The benefit which I expect from having him eat at a sort of boarding house is to have him see all sorts of characters and customs, for I do not send him travelling to see things but to see people of all sorts, and I had rather that he see the least of the counsellors of the Elector Palatine than the great tun at Heidelberg.

As for his exercises, they go without saying, with the single exception of dancing, which perhaps it would be better that he not take during his stay at Leipzig, for I confess that I have no conception of the graces that a dancing master of the Augsburg Confession could give him. Let us pass to manners. As for gaming and drink, you must do the utmost to correct them absolutely; show him the degrading baseness of these two vices, and if your representations have no effect, you will have to speak of them to those to whom he is closest in this country. In regard to women, it is not the same thing. It would be chimerical to hope that a young rogue full of health and vigor will keep his chastity. But all that you can and should do is to prevent such a debauch from becoming shameful and dishonorable, and from affecting his health. If it concerns the servant or the mistress of the house, it seems to me that you would do well to ignore it. If it is a matter of an affair with some woman of condition and *bon ton*, I admit that I should not interrupt it, for nothing refines a young man's manners so well as a connection with a woman of position in good company.

In regard to manners, it is absolutely necessary that his be gentle and polished; he already has some notions of what they are, and he is well aware of the necessity of pleasing, but as for the means, it is only a great knowledge of the world and of good company that can teach them to him. I therefore beg of you, Monsieur, have a very special eye to this head, so necessary to him, which you possess so well yourself. By his birth he will necessarily be in the House of Lords, and that before long, where I hope and even believe that he will be able to shine by his knowledge and his native talents, but I would not for the world that he be simply a *fat English Milord;* on the contrary I ardently desire that he shine at Court equally by his gentle and polished manners; in fine, that he be what they call in French "un parfaittement honnête et galant Homme," and in English, a *Gentleman*.

When he shall have finished his year at Leipzig, I would wish that he spend six months in grooming himself, in the places the least infested by his compatriots. They swarm always at Geneva and Lausanne; would Nancy, Lunéville, Lille, or Dijon in Burgundy be places of safety? You will know concerning that better than I, and I am sure that you will profit by that knowledge as far as you can.

After these eighteen months, he must come to Paris, the most dangerous place, as well as the most necessary, where he can make a considerable stay. So many debauched English on one side, so many Calypsos on the other! One must entrust him to providence, to his good sense, and to your counsels, which can do something, but not much. At Paris he cannot eat at a boarding house. He must eat at home when he is not invited elsewhere. Let him be very well lodged there, and let his equipage and his livery be of the finest. Let him have <at his own lodgings> the most fashionable dancing master, and let him have his other exercises, such as riding and fencing, at the <academy the most frequented by the young French nobility.> I would wish that he stay at least a whole year at Paris, to become a kind of naturalized Frenchman. After that he may go to southern France, merely to see Montpellier, Bordeaux, Toulouse, Aix-en-Provence, Lyons, etc., which will take little time. Let him see also those of the Swiss cantons which most merit his attention. Having dispatched all that, <I would have him go to the most considerable courts of Germany, not merely to see> the buildings, but to become acquainted with the sovereigns, ministers, customs, and manners. <As, for instance, he should stay at> the court of <Vienna four months; as long at> the court of <Berlin.> One <at Munich,> one at Mannheim, one <at Dresden.> <As for the> petty Highnesses of Germany, <he need only take them in his way and make a bow to> them in passing. In going through Flanders, which well deserves to be seen, he should stay five months at The Hague, to master the form of this complicated government, and to become acquainted with the ministers of all the courts of Europe. <His name will do him no hurt> in Holland.

You will without doubt be surprised, Monsieur, that Italy alone I do not name; the reason is that I do not wish him to go there at all. It is at present the seat of atheism, sodomy, and bad manners. The examples of the young Englishmen who return from thence, and also of those who do not return, such as Lord Tilney, Lord Cowper, etc., frighten me too much; those who escape the least damaged come back frivolous players of the clavichord or violin, or, indeed, ignorant *Virtuosi*. It is true that there are some very respectable remains of antiquity, but these are only things, and I do not send him travelling to see things but persons; and certainly these will not be the Italians.

If after having thoroughly seen the countries mentioned above, you can persuade him to make a tour of the north, I shall <be very glad;> I mean Petersburg, Stockholm, and Copenhagen, with which England will always have more or less to do. Seven or eight months will suffice for this tour, for I do not ask that he see these countries, but only these courts. He will soon be of a certain rank and he will have an estate, which will enable him to make use of his ability, and I think he has enough to distinguish himself in the world. But his travels must be directed to this object, before all others.

It is only a knowledge of the world at large and of good company which can polish a young man—I mean equally the company of women and men; and it is on this side that he lacks the most, like all the English. This is why I pray you, Monsieur, to give especial attention to this capital object. Push him into good society, make him take the tone of good company, be it even at the cost of his chastity.

After having left Leipzig he will be able to spend fifteen hundred pounds sterling a year, and in case of necessity, we shall not fall out over a few hundreds more.

You will both sign his drafts on your banker in London, to avoid all embarrassment.

You realize, Monsieur, that in his travels, and especially in Germany, a man who has not the finest châteaux in the world, and who cannot prove his thirty-two quarters like the Baron de Thunder-ten-tronckh, is not admitted to the tables of the higher nobility, wherefore one must let him go alone on his good faith.

Now that I have sufficiently explained my sentiments

concerning my boy, I finish my letter, already too long, without compliments, having given you undeniable proofs of the esteem and confidence with which I am very truly,

Monsieur,
Your most humble servant,
Chesterfield

Blackheath, the 26th July, 1771.

[XXVII]

My thoughts for the future Education of my Godson Philip Stanhope.¹¹¹

My principal object for the Boy is to have him educated in a way that may enable him hereafter to shine in Courts by his manners, and in Parliaments by his [*canc.:* learning; *interl.:* knowledge]. Nature has done her part [*interl.:* for him], and hitherto I have done mine, but as I have not the least reason to believe that I shall live long enough to complete his education, I leave these thoughts to those who will have the direction of it, not as positive rules, but as hints that may perhaps be of some use to them.

I would have him stay at Dr Dodd's till he will be near sixteen,¹¹² by which time he must have acquired more than a necessary share of Classical learning; for I am not of [*interl.:* the] opinion generally entertained in this Country, that Man lives by Greek and Latin alone, though it is obvious that he cannot understand those two dead languages correctly and minutely enough, to taste their finer and more delicate beautys.

Before he attains the age [*interl.:* of sixteen] I would have him transplanted at Geneva; I preferr that little Republick to any other place that I know of Academical exercises,¹¹³ Having seen more Genevans who had both learning and manners which are seldom United than from any other University, not excepting the two famous ones of Oxford and Cambridge.

There I would have him lodged and boarded in the House of a Professor *des belles lettres*. The constant conversation of the Professor will be full as instructive as his lectures.

I would wish him to be more particularly applyed to History both Antient and Modern, with its necessary companions Geography and Chronology.

To Rhetorick as much as possible, I mean, the liberal Rhetorick of Cicero and Quintilian.

To Logick, as little as possible, that is, no more than may enable him to Laugh at the ten Categorys, and at Syllogisms in BaraLipton.[114]

I would have him perfectioned in all the living languages, I mean Italian, Spanish, and German that he may be able to converse and negociate upon equal terms with people of all European Nations. For whoever converses or negociates in a language he is not perfectly Master of, not only seems to be, but really is below his [*interl.:* own] level.

The Law of Nature and Nations as treated by Burlamachi and Puffendorf (whom I greatly preferr to Grotius) should by no means be ommitted, and if a general notion of the *Ius Publicum imperii* be added so much the better.[115]

I do not mention Metaphysicks, being convinced that he now knows, and did know from his birth, as much of them, as any Man in the world ever did or ever will.[116]

Three years at Geneva will, I think, be fully sufficient to bring all this about. He will then be about nineteen when I would have him sent to Paris, and go for his exercises to that Academy which shall be then the most[117] frequented by young frenchmen of condition. I mean this more for the sake of his making proper French[118] acquaintances [*canc.:* amongst young Frenchmen], than for the exercises themselves which I suppose him to have been pretty well Master of during his stay at Geneva. I would wish him to stay at least a year at Paris, and then to begin his travels, but not in the manner that most of his Countrymen do, for I would have him pass as little of his time as possible upon the road, and as much as possible in the four or five capital Towns and Courts of Europe, such as Vienna, Munich, Dresden, Berlin and the Hague.[119] I insist upon his not going to Italy that foul sink of Illiberal Vices and manners, and from whence our young Countrymen return with at best the noble accomplishments, of Gimcrack *Virtuosi* or unskillfull Pipers and Fidlers, whizzing upon the Flute traversiere in a most ridiculous Attitude, or misleading an Orchestra upon a Harpsicord.[120] Musick though generally reckoned among the liberal Arts, is in my mind a very illiberal occupation for a Gentleman, and I never knew any great Composer or performer that had common sense, except that Amazing Phænomenon the king of Prussia.

Now the most difficult question arises, who shall have the care of him either as Governor or companion. I would by no means have that person, be an English Parson or a Scotch Doctor of Physick to introduce him into Low, and effectually to exclude him from all good company; But I should wish that some tolerably well bred Swiss [canc.: of; interl.: or] Genevan could be found out to have the general care of him, and even such a Person should be instructed not to pretend to go into all companys, but to let him often[121] go alone upon his parole.[122]

As he will be now of age and his own Master I can only recommend to him himself to visit the three Northern Courts of Russia, Sweden, and Denmark, not to reside long at any one, but only to review them. Six months will be sufficient for this purpose.

To conclude, as I began, I would have him qualifyed, by the graces and politeness of his manners, to shine in Courts, and by his knowledge to make a figure in Parliament.¹¹⁰ An uncommon Union, it is true of different Talents, but which those to whom I have recommended the superintendency of his Education, are [*canc.* most; *interl.*: more] likely to give him, than any other persons that I know.

¹¹¹ Plan II; see the Introduction, p. 11 and n. 15.

¹¹² Plan I begins: "As soon as he shall attain to the age of 15 I would have him exported and sent to Geneva. At that age the appetites begin to be busy, and I would much rather that their first Essays should be published abroad than at home, as probably they would be much less Illiberal and dangerous."

¹¹³ In Plan I the thought is elaborated: "The good order and Police of that little republick, prevent the Ostentation at least of scandalous and degrading vices. Vices there are no doubt as there are every where else, but *les mœurs* which are in fashion still, lessen in some degree their native turpitude. No Young Gentlemen there have an opportunity of distinguishing themselves as bungling Coachmen, or *too skillfull Jockeys*, nor of shining as Blackguards both in their dress and manners."

¹¹⁴ Baralipton: a mnemonic word in syllogistic logic.

¹¹⁵ Plan I is here more nearly like the letter to Deyverdun: "He should be thoroughly instructed in the Law of Nature and of Nations; and I could wish that Puffendorf and Burlamachi were his Manuals, rather than Grotius, who is a heap of Quotations, and very little to the purpose, from the Antient Poets; besides that he talks so absurdly of the divine right and absolute power of Kings, to make servile Court to Cardinal Richelieu and Lewis the thirteenth, that in the sequel of his book common sense and truth oblige him frequently to contradict himself."

¹¹⁶ A flower of rhetoric not unlike one in Plan III: "If he learns the first six books of Euclid, they will do him no harm, but if he should like them well enough to read the next six, I am sure they will do him no good." (Because Plan III was dictated, the original spelling and punctuation have not been retained.)

¹¹⁷ The two words "the most" were inserted in the margin, as the word immediately following comes at the beginning of a line.

¹¹⁸ Inserted in the margin, as the word immediately following comes at the beginning of a line.

¹¹⁹ Plan III is closer to the letter to Deyverdun: "From thence I would have him go to the most considerable Courts of Germany, not merely to see the palaces, the convents, and the great tun of Heidelberg, according to the custom of his countrymen, but to stay at each Court long enough to know and to be known by the most considerable persons of it; as for instance, he should stay at Vienna four months, at Berlin as long, three months at Dresden, two at Munich; as for the subordinate and Ecclesi-

astical Courts, he need only take them in his way, and make a bow to the respective potentates.

"I would have him stay a month at Brussels, in which time he will of course see all the considerable towns of Flanders.

"From thence I would have him go to Holland and stay four months at the Hague, where he will get acquainted with the Ministers of most of the Sovereigns of Europe, many of them better worth his acquaintance than those they represent."

In Plan I he was to "reside at the Hague at least five months, where his Name will do him no hurt."

[120] Plans I and III scarcely change the words.

Plan I: "It may perhaps be wondered at that in the course which I have charted out for his travels, I have not once mentioned Italy. My reason for it is, that I would upon no account have him in his Youth, go into that degenerate Country, which I look upon now to be the impure sink of Illiberal and shamefull vice and debauchery. The very best accomplishments that I have observed any of our Young Nobility bring home from thence, have been a very indifferent hand upon the Fiddle or the Harpsicord, and an expensive though bad taste of Pictures, Intaglias Cameos, with perhaps an Italian Strumpet into the bargain."

Plan III: "... but I would by no means have him go to Italy, which is at present the seat of all illiberal manners and vices, and from whence his young countrymen who escape the best, return either frivolous fiddlers and pipers, or ridiculous and ignorant virtuosi."

In his will Chesterfield declared: "I will and desire that he by no means go into Italy, which I look upon now to be the foul sink of illiberal manners and vices."

[121] Inserted in the margin, as the word immediately following came at the beginning of a line.

[122] In Plan III is the fruition of these ideas: "Now comes the most difficult point to be considered, who shall go with him? I would by no means have him sent under the care of an English parson, or a Scotch doctor of physic, as the fashion has been lately, nor in truth would I choose a native of these three Kingdoms, who are not in general formed to give the manners of a gentleman to a young man of quality, but I should wish that some Swiss, Genevan, or Frenchman could be found to accompany him. I have known many of those who have been men of good learning, and yet very near gentlemen. I know one M. Deyverdun of Lausanne, who is at present abroad with Sir Thomas Worseley, and who I think would answer this purpose; he has a great deal of useful polite learning, with almost the manners of a gentleman; but however, I would have this person, or any other who shall go abroad with the boy, informed that when his pupil shall be eighteen years old, he must not think of being inseparably joined to him like an unnatural birth, but let him go into good company alone, for what polite and gay company will admit a governor? It is this close adhesion of governors which hinders their pupils from

keeping good company, and which sinks them into that subordinate sort of company where their governors can only be admissible."

[128] Plan III: "It appears by what I have said that my view has always been and still is, in the education of this boy, to make him shine in Courts by the liberal manners and politeness of a gentleman, and in Parliaments by his knowledge and eloquence."

INDEX

Addison, Joseph, 3, 30
Ancaster, Peregrine, 3d Duke of, 59, 60n
Arnold, Mrs., 40

Bach, Johann Christian, 59, 60n
Bach, Johann Sebastian, 60n
Barbeyrac, Jean, 68n
Benet, Mr., 39
Black Prince. See Edward
Boswell, *Life of Johnson*, 4n, 5, 8n
Brühl, Friedrich Aloys, Count, 34, 35n, 47n
Burlamaqui, Jean-Jacques, 36, 58, 63, 68n, 70, 77, 79n

Candide, 13, 69n
Canons, 51n
Carlisle, Frederick Howard, 5th Earl of, 6
Carnarvon, Henry Howard Molyneux Herbert, 4th Earl of (editor of Chesterfield's *Letters to his Godson*), 1, 3n, 5, 6, 10, 13, 19n
Chandos, James Brydges, 3d Duke of, 51 and n
Chesterfield, Countess of, 37, 39, 51, 62n
Chesterfield House, 51n
Chesterfield, Philip Dormer Stanhope, 4th Earl of, *passim*; *Letters to A. C. Stanhope* (1817), 10, 11n, 12, 28n, 29n, 33n; *Letters to his Godson* (1890), 1, 3n, 5, 6, 19n; *Letters to his Son* (1774), 2, 5, 9, 31n, 33n, 53n; speech on reform of the calendar, 4, 27n; will, 6–7, 62n
Chesterfield, Philip Stanhope, 5th Earl of, *passim*
Cicero, 32
Claude Lorrain (*i.e.*, Claude Gelée), 61, 62n
Clodius, Christian August, 38, 40n, 46, 52, 54, 58

Common Sense, 3
Cowper, George Nassau, 3d Earl, 66, 69n, 73
Cromwell, Richard, 3
Cumberland, Henry Frederick, Duke of, 32, 33n

Dénoyer, 43
Devonshire, William Cavendish, 5th Duke of, 59, 60n
Deyverdun, Georges, 2, 8, 9, 10, 11, 13, 34, 37, 39, 41, 42, 43, 44, 46, 52, 54 and n, 56, 60, 80n; letter to, 63ff.
Dodd, Mrs., 44, 49
Dodd, Dr. William, 7, 8, 11n, 30, 34, 35n, 44, 48, 49, 50, 62n, 76
Dodsley, James, 2
Dodsley, Robert, 4
Dragon, 37, 39, 51
Drummond, Messrs., 39, 50, 61
Dryden, John, 30

Edward, the Black Prince, 20
Edward III, 20
Egremont, Countess of, 35n
Egremont, Sir George O'Brien Wyndham, 3d Earl of, 47n
Egremont House, 47
Einsiedel, Johann Georg, 34, 35n
Elizabeth, Queen, 22
Ernst, Mr., 34, 35n
Euclid, 79n

Fog's Journal, 3
Frederick the Great, 52, 53n, 54, 55, 56, 58, 78
Froissart, quoted, 63, 69n, 70, 79n

Garrick, David, 31
Gee, Miss, 40 and n
George III, 3
Gibbon, Edward, 8, 9 and n
Giordani, Tommaso, 59, 60n
Grotius, Hugo (Huig van Groot), 36, 58, 63, 68n, 69n, 70, 77, 79n

Heidelberg, the great tun of, 64, 69n, 79n
Henry V, 20
Henry VIII, 22
Hewit, Mr., 50
Horace, 32; quoted, 30, 31n
Hotham, Lady Gertrude, 62n

Johnson, Dr. Samuel, 3, 4, 8

Lorrain, Claude. See Claude Lorrain
Louis XIII, 79n

Marlborough, Sarah, Duchess of, 62n
Memmius, Gaius, 31 and n
Middleton, Lord, 9
Monconseil, Cécile-Thérèse (de Curzay), Mqse de, 69n
Morris, Capt. Charles, 58 and n

Newcastle, Thomas Pelham, 1st Duke of, 3, 4

Old England, 3
Osborne, Mr., 46
Ovid, *Metamorphoses*, 22, 29

Palatine, Elector, 64
Pitt, William, Earl of Chatham, 3
Pope, Alexander, 3, 30
Puffendorf, Baron Samuel von, 36, 58, 63, 68n, 70, 77, 79n

Richelieu, Cardinal, 36, 63, 68n, 70, 79n
Robert, M., 28 and n
Roberts, 40
Rous, Mr., 38

Saxony, Elector of, 46
Sophocles, 32

Stanhope. *See also* Chesterfield
Stanhope, Arthur Charles, 23, 26, 51n
Stanhope, Edwyn, 32, 33n
Stanhope, Eugenia, 2
Stanhope, Lady (widow of Sir William), 58 and n
Stanhope, Lovell, 51 and n
Stanhope, Margaret, 39, 40n, 50
Stanhope, Philip (Chesterfield's godson), *passim*
Stanhope, Philip (Chesterfield's illegitimate son), 5, 9, 68n
Stanhope, Walter (error for William?), 40
Stanhope, Sir William, 30, 31n, 32, 40n
Swift, Jonathan, 3

Thislethawit, Mr., 38, 40n
Thistlethwayte, Anne, 40n
Thistlethwayte, the Rev. Robert, 40n
Thunder-ten-tronckh, Baron, 68, 69n, 74
Tilney Hall, 32, 33n
Tilney, John, 2d Earl, 66, 69n, 73

Vallière, Mme de la, 62n
Virgil, quoted, 30, 31n
Voltaire, 53n. See also *Candide*

Waller, Edmund, 24, 26, 27
Walpole, Horace, 25n, 62n, 69n
Walpole, Sir Robert, 3
Walsh, James, 1, 2, 6, 14; notes by, 37, 39, 43, 47, 50, 60, 62
Walsh, Jemmy, 6
Warren, Dr. Richard, 37 and n, 43, 62
William the Conqueror, 20
Worseley, Sir Thomas, 80n

www.ingramcontent.com/pod-product-compliance
Lightning Source LLC
Chambersburg PA
CBHW021716230426
43668CB00008B/849